DEDICATION

This book is dedicated to
cookie monsters...everywhere!

IN APPRECIATION

A warm and heartfelt "Thanks" to
all our Gooseberry Patch family of friends who
reached deep into their cookie jars and
shared with us their yummiest cookie
recipes and sweetest cookie memories.

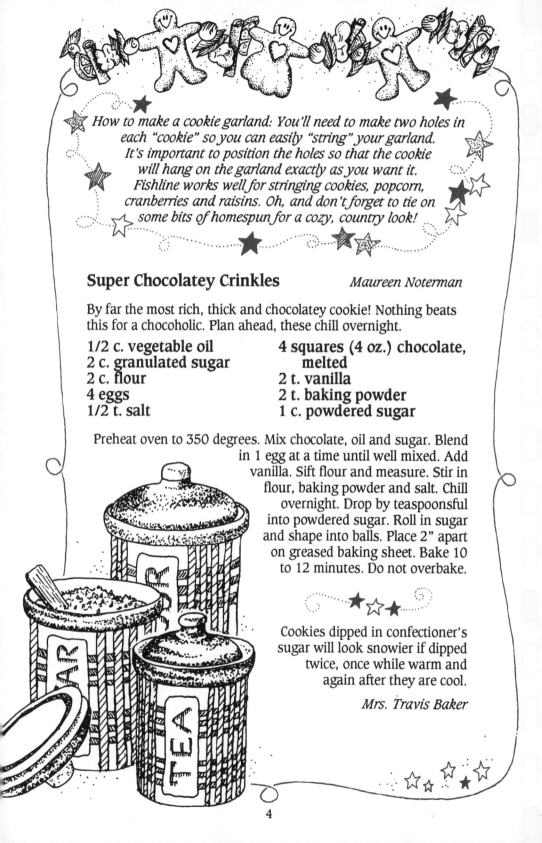

How to make a cookie garland: You'll need to make two holes in each "cookie" so you can easily "string" your garland. It's important to position the holes so that the cookie will hang on the garland exactly as you want it. Fishline works well for stringing cookies, popcorn, cranberries and raisins. Oh, and don't forget to tie on some bits of homespun for a cozy, country look!

Super Chocolatey Crinkles
Maureen Noterman

By far the most rich, thick and chocolatey cookie! Nothing beats this for a chocoholic. Plan ahead, these chill overnight.

1/2 c. vegetable oil	4 squares (4 oz.) chocolate,
2 c. granulated sugar	melted
2 c. flour	2 t. vanilla
4 eggs	2 t. baking powder
1/2 t. salt	1 c. powdered sugar

Preheat oven to 350 degrees. Mix chocolate, oil and sugar. Blend in 1 egg at a time until well mixed. Add vanilla. Sift flour and measure. Stir in flour, baking powder and salt. Chill overnight. Drop by teaspoonsful into powdered sugar. Roll in sugar and shape into balls. Place 2" apart on greased baking sheet. Bake 10 to 12 minutes. Do not overbake.

Cookies dipped in confectioner's sugar will look snowier if dipped twice, once while warm and again after they are cool.

Mrs. Travis Baker

Gooseberry Patch co. ®

A Country Store In Your Mailbox

Old-Fashioned Country Cookies

Yummy recipes, tips, traditions,
how-to's & sweet memories...
everything cookies!

Look for Vickie's & JoAnn's
favorite recipes and holiday hints
sprinkled throughout this book.

"A Country Store In Your Mailbox"®

Gooseberry Patch
600 London Road
Department BOOK
Delaware, OH 43015

★

1·800·85·GOOSE
1-800·854·6673

Copyright 1995, Gooseberry Patch 0-9632978-2-1
Eighth Printing, September, 2001

How to Subscribe

Would you like to receive
"A Country Store In Your Mailbox"®?
For a 2-year subscription to our 88-page
Gooseberry Patch catalog, simply send $3.00 to:

Gooseberry Patch
600 London Road
Department BOOK
Delaware, OH 43015

Banny's Southern Cream Cookies

Diann Fox

Five generations of women in our family have made these cookies...it's my great grandmother's recipe (Ol' Banny as we called her). The cookies were originally made with black walnuts because that is what Banny had, but you can substitute English walnuts or pecans with equally good results. Of course, that statement has led to many heated discussions, with each "nut" having its loyal following.

1 c. shortening	1 t. salt
2 c. sugar	3 t. baking powder
3 beaten eggs	1/2 t. baking soda
1 t. vanilla	1 1/2 c. black walnuts,
1 c. sour cream	chopped
5 c. flour	

Cream together the shortening and sugar. Add the eggs, vanilla and sour cream; mix well. Stir in the flour, salt, baking powder and baking soda to make a stiff dough. Add chopped nuts. Drop by teaspoonful onto greased cookie sheet. Mix 3 tablespoons sugar and 1 teaspoon cinnamon in a saucer. Grease the bottom of a jelly glass. Dip into the cinnamon/sugar and gently press the cookies to flatten the balls of dough. Bake at 350 degrees for 10 to 15 minutes or until centers are done. These cookies travel and freeze well. Makes 6 dozen.

Stained Glass Cookies

Here's how to make beautiful stained glass cookies. Using regular sugar cookie dough, roll out to a 1/4" thickness on a slightly floured board. With cookie cutters, cut dough into desired shapes. Trace a smaller version of cookie shape on dough leaving a 1/2" to 3/4" border of dough. Cut out and remove dough in center of cookies (to save time, and avoid tracing, use a smaller version cookie cutter to cut out the center). Place on baking sheets lined with foil. Then take five rolls of crushed lifesavers or lifesaver holes and spoon candy into the center of the cookies. Bake until candy is melted and cookie is slightly brown. Cool completely before removing from pan.

Michele Urdahl

Congo Bars

Tracy McHugh

"Congo Bars" were my brothers' and my favorite. Grandma baked a roasting pan-full each time we visited and (if they made it that far) stored them in a big round tin, kept accessible in a drawer. One time she had just pulled them out of the oven and told my older brother and I that we could help ourselves, she had to go to the store. By the time she returned, we had eaten two-thirds of the pan! She never said a word. Aren't grandmothers wonderful?

2/3 c. butter or margarine, melted
1 lb. brown sugar
3 eggs
1 t. vanilla
2 3/4 c. sifted flour
2 1/2 t. baking powder
1/2 t. salt
1 c. coarsely chopped nuts (optional)
12 oz. semi-sweet chocolate chips

In a large bowl or pan (after melting), combine margarine and brown sugar. Add eggs one at a time, beating well after each. Add vanilla. Sift together dry ingredients and add to sugar mixture. Add nuts and chocolate chips. Pour into greased, shallow roasting pan. Bake at 350 degrees for 22-25 minutes (don't overbake).

Pineapple Cookies

Doris Stegner
Gooseberry Patch

1 c. brown sugar
1 c. granulated sugar
1 c. shortening
2 eggs
20 oz. can crushed pineapple, drained
1 1/2 t. vanilla
4 c. flour
1/2 t. salt
1 1/2 t. soda
1/2 t. baking powder

Stir vanilla into crushed pineapple. Cream shortening, sugar and eggs. Add pineapple and stir until well blended. Sift flour, salt, soda and baking powder together; then gradually stir into batter (use all 4 cups of flour). When thoroughly mixed drop by spoonfuls onto cookie sheet. Bake at 350 degrees for 12 to 15 minutes.

Butterscotch Cookies

Kathy Grashoff

1 c. shortening
3/4 c. brown sugar
3/4 c. white sugar
2 eggs, beaten
1 t. hot water
1 t. vanilla
1 1/2 c. sifted flour

1 t. salt
1 t. soda
2 c. oatmeal
1 c. chopped nuts
   (optional)
24 oz. pkg.
   butterscotch chips

Mix shortening, brown and white sugars, eggs, hot water and vanilla. Add flour, salt and soda, stirring well. Then add oatmeal, nuts and butterscotch chips. Drop by teaspoonsful on a cookie sheet. Bake at 350 degrees for 10 to 15 minutes.

Our veterinarian is sort of the "James Herriott of Juneau." During a visit he recounted the story of a kindly client who had made Christmas "cookies" for his dogs. They were, of course, mostly barley, wheat flour, yeast and other high-fiber ingredients. He took them to his cabin on Admiralty Island as special treats for his beloved hounds. Some weeks later, he gave some visiting "friends-of-a-friend" permission to use the cabin for a week. On his next trip over, he found a note from the people who had visited. It said, "Thanks so much for the use of the cabin, and for the wonderful cookies you left us. Unfortunately, we were only able to stay a few days since we all seemed to have some sort of digestive upset." The "doggie cookie jar" was, of course, empty.

Catherine Brown

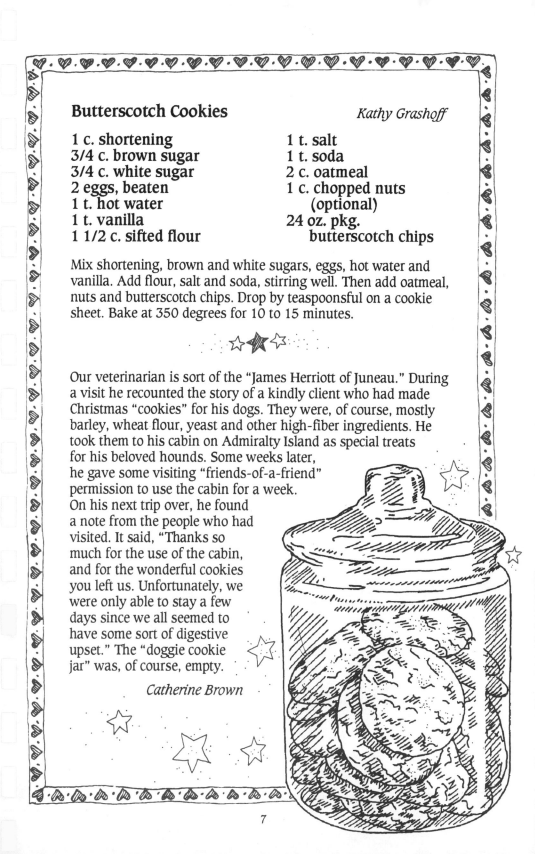

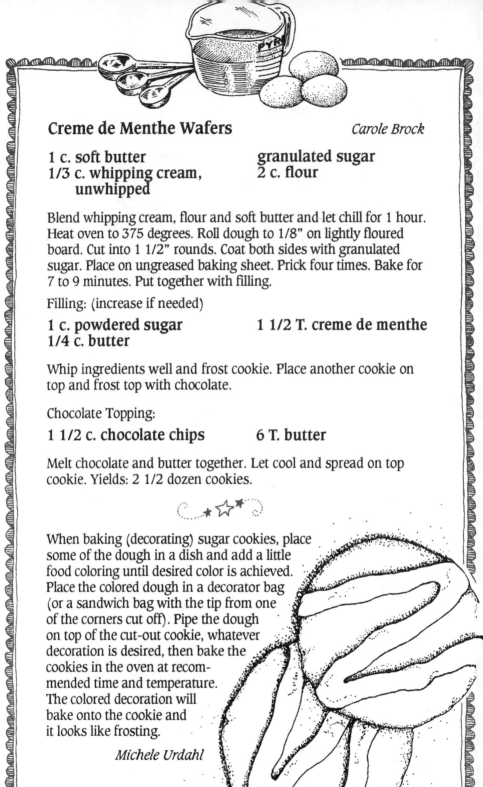

Creme de Menthe Wafers
Carole Brock

1 c. soft butter
1/3 c. whipping cream,
   unwhipped

granulated sugar
2 c. flour

Blend whipping cream, flour and soft butter and let chill for 1 hour. Heat oven to 375 degrees. Roll dough to 1/8" on lightly floured board. Cut into 1 1/2" rounds. Coat both sides with granulated sugar. Place on ungreased baking sheet. Prick four times. Bake for 7 to 9 minutes. Put together with filling.

Filling: (increase if needed)

1 c. powdered sugar
1/4 c. butter

1 1/2 T. creme de menthe

Whip ingredients well and frost cookie. Place another cookie on top and frost top with chocolate.

Chocolate Topping:

1 1/2 c. chocolate chips

6 T. butter

Melt chocolate and butter together. Let cool and spread on top cookie. Yields: 2 1/2 dozen cookies.

When baking (decorating) sugar cookies, place some of the dough in a dish and add a little food coloring until desired color is achieved. Place the colored dough in a decorator bag (or a sandwich bag with the tip from one of the corners cut off). Pipe the dough on top of the cut-out cookie, whatever decoration is desired, then bake the cookies in the oven at recommended time and temperature. The colored decoration will bake onto the cookie and it looks like frosting.

Michele Urdahl

8

Pizzles (Italian Waffle Cookies) *Deb Damari-Tull*

My grandfather left Rome, Italy, as a teenager. After arriving in the United States, he met and fell in love with a 4'6" spitfire of a woman (my grandmother) also Italian, but born in the U.S. The years that followed were filled with love and an abundance of Italian delicacies. It simply would not be a holiday without these cookies. Now-a-days, there is a modern electric pizzle iron available at Italian grocers and kitchen supply stores. Wonderfully, they make two cookies at a time. In the "old days" my little "Nona" stood over the gas flame of her stove holding an old, cast iron pizzlemaker with a long handle, browning one side of the cookie at a time. You made one cookie at a time and the iron weighed about 5 pounds! I now have the iron in my kitchen, but needless to say, I use my electric one. You can imagine how good these cookies are for someone to go through such a process for one cookie. Especially infuriating was the fact that her four sons and eventually her grandchildren would come into the kitchen and grab a 4" stack at a time and gobble! My little Nona passed away 3 years ago Christmas Day, but her traditions and loving ways will be carried on in this family forever!

6 eggs
3 1/2 c. flour
1 1/2 c. sugar
2 sticks butter or
   margarine, melted

4 t. baking powder
2 T. plus anise and/or
vanilla flavoring
anise seeds (optional)

Beat eggs until foamy. Add sugar and melted margarine. Follow with other ingredients, mixing thoroughly. Place 1 teaspoonful on each side of iron and cook until delicately browned. Lay flat until cooled. Yum!

Tie cookie cutters onto a raffia or ribbon swag...use for a cute kitchen decoration. Use lots of raffia and a good many cutters. Hang lengthwise.

Patricia Husek

9

Mom's Gingerbread Cookies
Michele Urdahl

When I was little, Mom and I used to bake gingerbread men together at Christmas time. I remember peeking through the oven door, just waiting for one of them to get up off the pan, just like the stories!

1/2 c. shortening
2 1/2 c. all-purpose flour
1/2 c. sugar
1/2 c. molasses
1 egg

1 t. baking soda
1 t. ground ginger
1/2 t. ground cinnamon
1/2 t. ground cloves

Beat shortening until softened. Add about half the flour, the sugar, molasses, egg, baking soda, ginger, cinnamon and cloves. Beat until thoroughly combined. Stir in remaining flour. Divide dough in half. Cover dough and chill for 3 hours, or until easily handled. Roll each half of the dough to a 1/8" to 1/4" thickness. Cut out man with cutter. Put on an ungreased cookie sheet and bake at 375 degrees for 5 to 6 minutes or until edges are firm. Ice with powdered sugar icing.

Powdered Sugar Icing:

1 c. powdered sugar, sifted
1/4 t. vanilla
1 T. milk

Mix all ingredients together using about one tablespoon milk or enough until spreading consistency is achieved.

☆ ★ ☆ ★ ☆

Cookies, cookies, cookies...my favorite, favorite, favorite! Fun to bake and fun to eat! Nothing short of the aroma of fresh baked bread or fresh perked coffee gives us such pleasure.

Pat Akers

★ ☆ ★

Brown Sugar Spice Cookies

Sandra Bowman

These cookies look really nice when you use a leaf-shaped cookie cutter, gingerbread man or pumpkin cutter because the dough is a pretty brown color. They are so delicious, no icing is needed.

1 1/2 c. softened butter
2 c. packed brown sugar
1 egg
4 c. all-purpose flour
2 t. cinnamon

1 t. ground nutmeg
1/2 t. ground cloves
1/4 t. baking
   soda

Cream butter and brown sugar, add egg. Beat until light and fluffy. Stir flour with spices and soda, add to creamed mixture; mix well. Cover and chill until firm, about 2 hours. On floured surface roll dough to 1/8" thickness. Cut into shapes with cookie cutters. Place on ungreased cookie sheet. Bake in 350 degree oven 8 to 10 minutes or until lightly browned. Makes 6 dozen cookies.

Stencilled Cookies

Stencilled cookies are wonderful and easy to make. Using waxed paper, cut out your own pattern. Just fold paper into quarters, then again in half, making a triangle. Cut shapes out of both folds and point, then unfold. Now place it on top of your baked cookie, sift any type of sugar desired (colored or powdered) over stencil.

Michele Urdahl

Walnut Tartlets

Judy Voster

These cookies are so light and melt-in-your-mouth that nobody can eat just one. Enjoy!

Cream Cheese Pastry:

1/2 c. butter or, margarine softened	1 T. sugar
	1 1/3 c. flour
3 oz. pkg. cream cheese, softened	pinch of salt

Walnut Filling:

2 eggs	1 T. butter or margarine, melted
1/2 c. sugar	
1/2 c. light or dark corn syrup	1/2 t. vanilla
	1 c. finely chopped walnuts

To make pastry: In a large bowl combine butter, cream cheese and sugar; stir until well blended. Add flour and salt, stir until thoroughly combined. Roll dough into 1" balls. Press evenly into bottom and sides of 1 3/4"x1" miniature muffin cups. Refrigerate.

To make filling: In a medium bowl beat eggs slightly. Stir in sugar, corn syrup, butter, vanilla and walnuts. Spoon 1 tablespoon mixture into each pastry-lined cup. Bake in a 350 degree oven for 20 to 25 minutes or until lightly browned. Cool in pans for 5 minutes. Remove and cool completely on a wire rack. Store in tightly covered containers. Makes about 2 dozen.

★ ☆ ★

If you have large numbers of children (i.e. scouting groups or large family gatherings) helping with the traditional cookie baking and are running low on cookie cutters, the metal edge off discarded boxes of plastic wrap and waxed paper boxes can be used to create instant, one-of-a-kind cookie cutters. Just bend into desired shapes!

Judy Hand

Chunky Chippers

Sandy Bessingpas

This is my favorite chocolate chip cookie recipe. I love the combination of chocolate and peanut butter.

2 c. flour
1 t. baking soda
1/2 c. margarine
1/2 c. chunky
   peanut butter
2 eggs

1 c. sugar
1/2 c. packed brown sugar
1 t. vanilla
1 T. water
1 c. chocolate chips

Beat sugars, margarine and peanut butter. Add eggs, water and vanilla, mixing well. Add dry ingredients, blend well. Stir in chocolate chips. Drop by teaspoonsful on cookie sheet. Bake at 350 degrees for 12 to 14 minutes. Makes 6 dozen.

Cinnamon Ornaments

Mix 3/4 to 1 cup of smooth applesauce with one 4.12 ounce bottle of ground cinnamon (adding applesauce a little bit at a time) to form a stiff dough. Roll out to a 1/4" thickness. Cut with cookie cutters. Make a hole on each cut-out for a ribbon by using a straw to punch out a hole. Carefully put on a rack to dry. Let air dry for several days, turning occasionally. Makes 12 ornaments (depending on size of cutters used). Garlands can also be made with your cut-out shapes.

Michele Urdahl

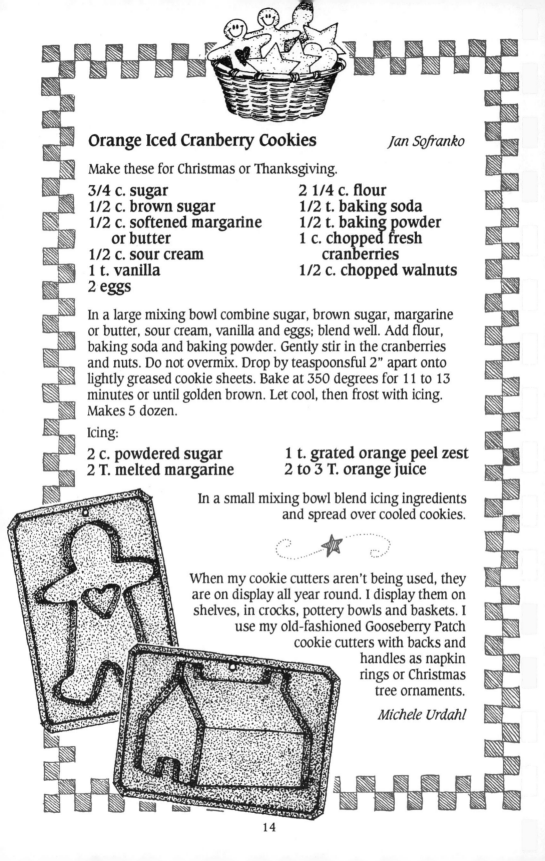

Orange Iced Cranberry Cookies

Jan Sofranko

Make these for Christmas or Thanksgiving.

3/4 c. sugar
1/2 c. brown sugar
1/2 c. softened margarine
   or butter
1/2 c. sour cream
1 t. vanilla
2 eggs

2 1/4 c. flour
1/2 t. baking soda
1/2 t. baking powder
1 c. chopped fresh
   cranberries
1/2 c. chopped walnuts

In a large mixing bowl combine sugar, brown sugar, margarine or butter, sour cream, vanilla and eggs; blend well. Add flour, baking soda and baking powder. Gently stir in the cranberries and nuts. Do not overmix. Drop by teaspoonsful 2" apart onto lightly greased cookie sheets. Bake at 350 degrees for 11 to 13 minutes or until golden brown. Let cool, then frost with icing. Makes 5 dozen.

Icing:

2 c. powdered sugar
2 T. melted margarine

1 t. grated orange peel zest
2 to 3 T. orange juice

In a small mixing bowl blend icing ingredients and spread over cooled cookies.

When my cookie cutters aren't being used, they are on display all year round. I display them on shelves, in crocks, pottery bowls and baskets. I use my old-fashioned Gooseberry Patch cookie cutters with backs and handles as napkin rings or Christmas tree ornaments.

Michele Urdahl

Chocolate Cookies

Jackie Sholes

1 c. shortening
1 c. sugar
3 c. brown sugar
4 eggs
2 c. milk
6 c. flour

8 T. cocoa
2 t. baking soda
1 T. raspberry liqueur
1 c. nutmeats
1 c. raisins
(I soak mine in rum)

Cream shortening and the sugars. Add the eggs. Add the milk alternating with the flour, cocoa and baking soda. Then add the liqueur, nutmeats and raisins, mixing well. Drop by teaspoonsful onto cookie sheet. Bake at 350 degrees for 10 to 12 minutes.

Frosting:

3 T. butter
1 square chocolate
2 T. cream
1 egg
1 1/2 c. confectioner's sugar
1 T. raspberry liqueur

Melt butter, chocolate and cream. Cool and add egg, confectioner's sugar and liqueur. Frost cookies.

✿ ★☆★ ✿

If your cookies get too brown on the bottom no matter what you do (air-cushion sheet, lowering oven temperature, whatever), try this idea. Invest in two heavy gauge aluminum jelly roll pans of good quality. Use them only for cookies (or jelly rolls, of course) and keep them clean and bright. Also, be sure to let your pans cool off between batches so that your dough doesn't spread or pre-bake. Bake only one sheet at a time for best quality. Always remove your cookies promptly from the cookie sheet to a cooling rack.

Catherine Brown

15

Favorite "Meeting" Bar

Dorothy Hanford

This cookie has gone to many meetings (as it makes a goodly amount). Depending on the size of the bars, one recipe will provide 4 to 6 dozen and the recipe is always requested.

1 c. shortening
1/2 c. sugar plus 1 c.
2 1/2 c. flour
1 egg yolk

1/4 t. salt
1/2 c. preserves
4 egg whites
1 t. vanilla

Cream shortening, 1/2 cup sugar and egg yolk. Add salt and flour. Spread on ungreased 12"x18" cookie sheet. Spread preserves (apricot-pineapple is magnificent) on top and sprinkle with 3/4 cup chopped nuts if desired. Beat egg whites until foamy and gradually beat in the cup of sugar. Beat until stiff and add vanilla. Spread over preserves. Bake at 350 degrees for 35 to 40 minutes. Let cool and cut into bars.

Salt Dough Ornaments

1/2 c. salt
2 c. flour
3/4 c. boiling water

Place salt in a bowl, pour boiling water over salt and stir; then let cool. Add flour (all at once) and mix well by forming a ball and kneading the dough until it is smooth, soft and workable. Roll out dough on a floured surface if necessary. Cut out whatever shapes desired. Then carefully insert a piece of wire into the top of the ornament, pushing the long end into the center of the ornament until loop rests on the top of the shape. Transfer completed ornaments, with wire onto baking sheet covered with tin foil. Place in a 150 to 200 degree oven and bake until ornaments become completely hard. When cool, paint ornaments or personalize with markers. To prevent ornaments from bulging, use a toothpick to prick small holes into the shapes before baking. Makes many ornaments.

Michele Urdahl

Chocolate Chip Cream Cheese Bars *Rosina Robinson*

About 8 years ago I retired from the "world of business" and went back to my first profession as a nurse in the operating room of a small community hospital. What a wonderful group I worked with! Christmas rolled around and goodies baked by my co-workers appeared on almost a daily basis. Then came a day I'll never forget. Yummy chocolate chip cheese cake bars...they were heavenly! We all wanted to know who baked them, but no one would confess and take the praise. Then he owned up to it...gruff, short-tempered, cigarette-smoking, coffee-drinking, pool-playing Hal, an ex-Army air corp medic. Even though Hal is no longer with us, his Chocolate Chip Cream Cheese Bars remain an all-time favorite!

1 roll refrigerated chocolate chip cookie dough
1 large cream cheese (the real thing, not imitation or light)

1 egg
1/2 to 3/4 c. sugar

Pat out 1/2 of the dough into a 9"x9" pan. Mix cream cheese, egg and sugar until smooth. Spread over dough. Top with remaining cookie dough. Bake until toothpick comes out clean at temperature recommended on the dough. Quick, easy and yummy!

☆ ★ ☆ ★ ☆

For perfectly shaped round cookies, pack homemade refrigerator cookie dough into clean 6 oz. juice cans (don't remove the bottoms), and freeze dough. Thaw cookie dough about 15 minutes; then open bottom of can and push up, using the top edge as a cutting guide.

Barbara Bargdill
Gooseberry Patch

Speedy Little Devils

Marty Darling

1 devils food cake mix	7 oz. jar marshmallow
1 stick margarine	cream
1 egg	1/2 c. peanut butter

Melt margarine and add dry cake mix. Add egg and stir until well mixed. Put approximately 1/2 of the mixture on the bottom of an ungreased 13"x9" pan. Pat down evenly. Combine peanut butter and marshmallow cream and spread over bottom layer. Crumble remaining cake mixture over the top and bake 20 minutes at 350 degrees. Cool and cut into bars.

I have used my cookie cutters in many ways. One Christmas, I decorated our huge tree with cutters tied with red ribbons. I used the miniature cutters as napkin rings on the table, I placed some of the miniatures amongst the greenery and berries in our center-piece on the table, and for each family member (a total of 8 that year) I baked a special batch of cookies, wrapped them, and tied a cutter on each of their Christmas boxes. It was all very colorful and enjoyed by all.

Rhonda Krogman

Since I collect cookie cutters, I like to display them in a wooden bowl at Christmas with pine sprigs and cones, or in a pottery bowl or large glass cannister.

Joyce Newburn

Pile cookie cutters into an old wooden bowl or depression glass bowl or basket. Display for an instant antique decoration. Accent with greenery for the holidays.

Patricia Husek

18

Monster Cookies

Marty Darling

3 eggs
1 1/2 c. brown sugar
1 c. white sugar
3/4 t. vanilla
1 t. light corn syrup
2 t. baking soda

1 stick margarine, softened
1 1/2 c. peanut butter
4 1/2 c. oatmeal
2/3 c. chocolate chips
2/3 c. candy coated
  chocolate pieces

Mix in order. Drop by teaspoonsful onto ungreased cookie sheet. Flatten slightly. Bake at 350 degrees for 10 minutes.

Summer Snowballs

Jane Granger

Fill a glass canning jar with these cookies and give to a special friend, neighbor or shut-in. Great for the holidays, all you have to do is write a little note and tie a ribbon around the jar.

1 c. flour
1 t. baking powder
1/4 t. salt
2 T. butter
2 squares unsweetened
  chocolate

1 c. white sugar
2 eggs
1/2 c. chopped walnuts

Mix flour, baking powder and salt together. Melt butter and chocolate; let cool to lukewarm. Beat in sugar and eggs, one at a time; continue to beat for 1 minute. Stir flour mixture and walnuts together until blended. Add chocolate mixture to flour mixture, blending well. Chill until firm enough to shape into balls. Roll in powdered sugar. Bake at 300 degrees for 18 to 20 minutes. Makes 3 1/2 dozen.

Here's a clever idea for making biscuits. Open a refrigerated tube of biscuit dough, roll out to 1/2" thickness. Using your favorite cookie cutters, cut out 8 to 10 biscuits. Brush with melted butter and sprinkle on poppy or sesame seeds. Bake at 400 degrees for 10 to 12 minutes.

Holiday Cookie Tree

I've come up with a fun cookie tree decoration idea for a child's party or a holiday get together. For Halloween parties I have hung ghost and bat shapes from the limbs of our tree; for Christmas I've made star, bell and tree shaped cookies, then have given them away at our Christmas party. For my daughter's birthday, I wrapped the dowels in a bright print and hung animal shaped cookies to go along with the Noah's Ark theme. The children enjoyed taking the cookies home at the end of the party! Here's what you'll need:

4 wooden dowels (one each, measuring 8", 12", 16", and 20" with 1/4" diameters)
1- 34" dowel (for the "trunk" with a 1/2" diameter)
fabric strips (holiday designs or country prints)
tacky glue
terra cotta pot (measuring 8" in diameter)
jelly beans or pebbles

Cut strips of fabric approximately 2"Wx6"L. You can use different patterns to create a patchwork effect, experimenting to see what you like best. Starting at the top of the tree, secure fabric strip with a dab of tacky glue and begin to wrap dowel. At the end of each fabric strip, use a small dab of glue to secure and then start wrapping a new fabric strip. First attach the 8" rod across the 34" rod approximately 5-1/2" from the top, then attach the 12", 16" and 20" rods, spacing each about 5-1/2" apart. When attaching the branches, criss-cross your fabric to hold the branches to the trunk securely. Wrap the tree until there is no wood exposed. Taking the terra cotta pot, put some glue in the drainage hole at the bottom and insert the end of the trunk in the hole, adding pebbles or jelly beans to support the trunk. Now you're ready to decorate your tree with cookies by tying them on with ribbon, raffia or jute. Hint: So you can easily move your cookie tree from one container to another, put the trunk in a 1 lb. coffee can and fill with cement. Now it's easy to change containers giving your tree a whole new look, simply camouflage the coffee can by setting your tree down into an old sugar maple bucket, salt-glazed crock or basket!

Cara Killingsworth

Angie's Chocolate Chip Oatmeal Cookies

Angie Yanchik

1/2 c. butter or margarine, softened
3/4 c. packed dark brown sugar
1 egg or 2 egg whites
1 t. vanilla
1 heaping c. all-purpose flour

1/2 rounded t. baking soda
1/2 level t. salt
1 c. semi-sweet chocolate chips
1 c. quick cooking oatmeal, dry
3/4 c. coarsely chopped walnuts

In a large bowl cream together butter and sugar. Add egg or egg white, beat well. Stir in vanilla, blending well. In a separate bowl, combine flour, baking soda and salt, mix together well. Add flour mixture, slowly, to butter mixture, combining well. Add chocolate chips, oatmeal and walnuts to the batter, mix well. Refrigerate at least 3 hours or overnight. This batter will keep in refrigerator (tightly covered) for a week. When ready to bake, pre-heat oven to 375 degrees. Grease and flour two cookie sheets. Form 1" balls and place 1" apart on the cookie sheets (12 balls per cookie sheet). Place both cookie sheets in oven and bake for 15 minutes. After the first 8 minutes switch and rotate trays, then finish baking 7 minutes or until done (dark brown).

Here's a neat trick. Chill and slice stick butter or margarine. Cut each piece with your miniature heart cookie cutter. Place on a pretty glass tray or 2 hearts on each bread dish. Your guests will rave, but you know the secret is simple!

Victoria McLaughlin

To test baking soda for freshness, pour 1/4 cup hot water over 1/2 teaspoon of soda. If it doesn't bubble actively, it's too old!

Mary McCullough

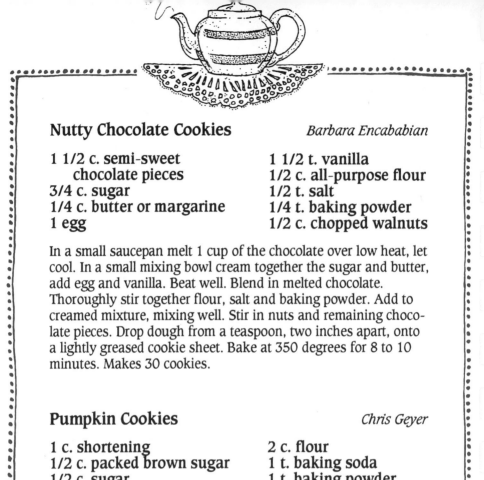

Nutty Chocolate Cookies
Barbara Encababian

1 1/2 c. semi-sweet
   chocolate pieces
3/4 c. sugar
1/4 c. butter or margarine
1 egg

1 1/2 t. vanilla
1/2 c. all-purpose flour
1/2 t. salt
1/4 t. baking powder
1/2 c. chopped walnuts

In a small saucepan melt 1 cup of the chocolate over low heat, let cool. In a small mixing bowl cream together the sugar and butter, add egg and vanilla. Beat well. Blend in melted chocolate. Thoroughly stir together flour, salt and baking powder. Add to creamed mixture, mixing well. Stir in nuts and remaining chocolate pieces. Drop dough from a teaspoon, two inches apart, onto a lightly greased cookie sheet. Bake at 350 degrees for 8 to 10 minutes. Makes 30 cookies.

Pumpkin Cookies
Chris Geyer

1 c. shortening
1/2 c. packed brown sugar
1/2 c. sugar
1 c. mashed cooked
   pumpkin
1 egg
1 t. vanilla

2 c. flour
1 t. baking soda
1 t. baking powder
1 t. cinnamon
1/2 t. salt
1 c. chopped nuts

Cream shortening and sugars well. Add pumpkin, egg and vanilla; mix well. Sift dry ingredients, add to creamed mixture and blend well. Stir in nuts. Drop onto greased cookie sheets. Bake at 350 degrees for 10 to 12 minutes. Cool and frost.

Penuche Frosting:

3 T. butter
1/2 c. firmly packed
   brown sugar

1/4 c. milk
2 c. powdered sugar

Combine butter and sugar in a saucepan; bring to a boil. Cook and stir for 1 minute or until slightly thickened. Cool slightly. Add milk, beat until smooth. Stir in powdered sugar to make a spreading consistency. Spread on cookies.

Sugar Plum Raisin Squares

Barbara Elliott

These are a wonderful and easy addition to a holiday cookie tray. These bars are also relatively inexpensive to make, an added bonus around the holidays.

1/2 c. butter or margarine
1/4 c. brown sugar, packed

1/4 t. salt
1 c. flour

Mix ingredients and pat on the bottom of a 13"x9" pan. Bake at 325 degrees for 15 minutes. While bottom is baking, combine:

2 eggs
1 c. brown sugar, packed
1 t. vanilla
1/4 t. salt
2 T. flour
1/2 t. baking powder

1 c. coarsely chopped
   nuts (pecans or
   English walnuts)
3/4 c. raisins
1/4 t. ground ginger

Pour mixture on hot crust. Bake for an additional 20 minutes. Cool in pan on wire rack. Cut into bars before completely cooled.

At Christmastime I put together gingerbread families for all my grandchildren. I have a Mama, Papa, sister and brothers, along with pet bears or dogs and each one has a tiny red satin ribbon tied around its neck. I pack these "families" in Christmas tins or colorful small paper bags. Who says children shouldn't play with their food?

Tamara Gruber

Christmas Cut-Out Cow Cookies *Maureen Noterman*

What makes this cookie so cute is the fact that it's a brown gingerbread roll cookie. To create a cow (or pig) just add "white spots". A whole batch of the same animal sure looks cute on a cookie tray!

1 c. butter
1 c. sugar
1 egg
1 c. dark molasses
2 T. vinegar
5 c. flour (or slightly more)

1 1/2 t. baking soda
1/2 t. salt
2 t. ginger
1 t. cinnamon
1 t. cloves

Cream butter and sugar. Add egg, beat well. Add molasses and vinegar. Sift together flour, soda, and salt; add to creamed mixture along with the ginger, cinnamon and cloves. Roll with a bit of flour to 1/4" thickness. Use animal cookie cutters to cut out desired animal shape. Bake at 350 degrees for 10 to 12 minutes.

Frosting:

2 egg whites
2 1/2 c. powdered sugar

1/4 c. white syrup

Beat the egg whites to soft peaks. Add powdered sugar, then add the syrup. Beat for one minute.

If you want to make two-toned cookies, make a batch of sugar cookie dough and chocolate cookie dough. First roll out sugar cookie dough, add tiny chocolate dough balls here and there, roll out again and it's ready to cut. Fun to make spotted cows, pigs, kitties, dogs and bunnies!

Scrumptious Chocolate Layer Bars
Mary Dungan

2 c. semi-sweet
   chocolate chips
8 oz. cream cheese
5.3 oz. can evaporated milk
1 c. chopped walnuts
1/2 t. almond extract

3 c. unsifted flour
1 1/2 c. granulated sugar
1 t. baking powder
1 c. softened butter
2 eggs

Combine chocolate chips, cream cheese and evaporated milk in sauce pan at low heat, stirring constantly until smooth. Remove from heat. Stir in nuts and extract, blending well. Set aside to cool. In a large bowl, by hand or with a blender, blend flour, sugar, baking powder, butter and eggs until it resembles coarse crumbs. Press 1/2 of mixture into a greased 13"x9" pan. Spread cooled chocolate mixture over first layer, then sprinkle remaining mixture over all. Bake for 35 to 40 minutes at 375 degrees. Cool, cut and store.

Cookie Lollipops

Here's an easy way to make kid-pleasing party treats or favors. Following your favorite chocolate chip cookie recipe, drop heaping tablespoonsful onto baking sheet (leave extra room in between cookies for spreading). Insert a wooden craft stick into the center of each cookie and flatten dough slightly. At this point, colored sugar or sprinkles can be pressed gently into the dough. Bake following directions until edges are browned. Cool slightly and remove from cookie sheet. When completely cooled, wrap cookie pops in different colored plastic wrap. Tie bows on, mixing or matching curling ribbon, leaving plenty of curly tendrils. These pretty cookie pops look just great at a party! They are also great sellers at bake sales.

Linda Lee

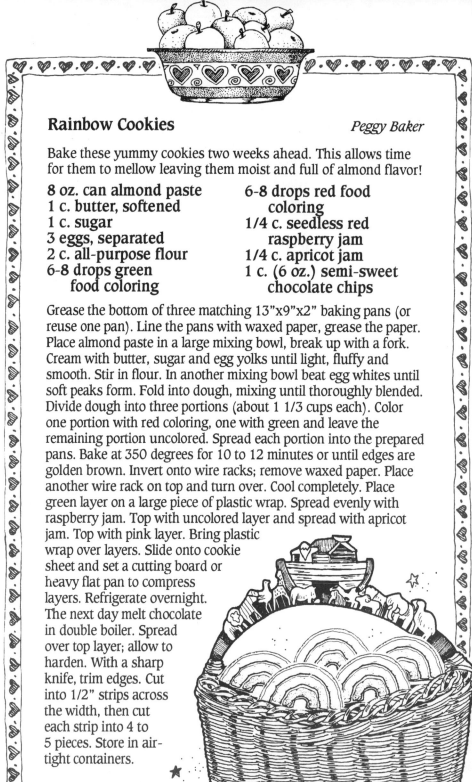

Rainbow Cookies

Peggy Baker

Bake these yummy cookies two weeks ahead. This allows time for them to mellow leaving them moist and full of almond flavor!

8 oz. can almond paste
1 c. butter, softened
1 c. sugar
3 eggs, separated
2 c. all-purpose flour
6-8 drops green
   food coloring

6-8 drops red food
   coloring
1/4 c. seedless red
   raspberry jam
1/4 c. apricot jam
1 c. (6 oz.) semi-sweet
   chocolate chips

Grease the bottom of three matching 13"x9"x2" baking pans (or reuse one pan). Line the pans with waxed paper, grease the paper. Place almond paste in a large mixing bowl, break up with a fork. Cream with butter, sugar and egg yolks until light, fluffy and smooth. Stir in flour. In another mixing bowl beat egg whites until soft peaks form. Fold into dough, mixing until thoroughly blended. Divide dough into three portions (about 1 1/3 cups each). Color one portion with red coloring, one with green and leave the remaining portion uncolored. Spread each portion into the prepared pans. Bake at 350 degrees for 10 to 12 minutes or until edges are golden brown. Invert onto wire racks; remove waxed paper. Place another wire rack on top and turn over. Cool completely. Place green layer on a large piece of plastic wrap. Spread evenly with raspberry jam. Top with uncolored layer and spread with apricot jam. Top with pink layer. Bring plastic wrap over layers. Slide onto cookie sheet and set a cutting board or heavy flat pan to compress layers. Refrigerate overnight. The next day melt chocolate in double boiler. Spread over top layer; allow to harden. With a sharp knife, trim edges. Cut into 1/2" strips across the width, then cut each strip into 4 to 5 pieces. Store in air-tight containers.

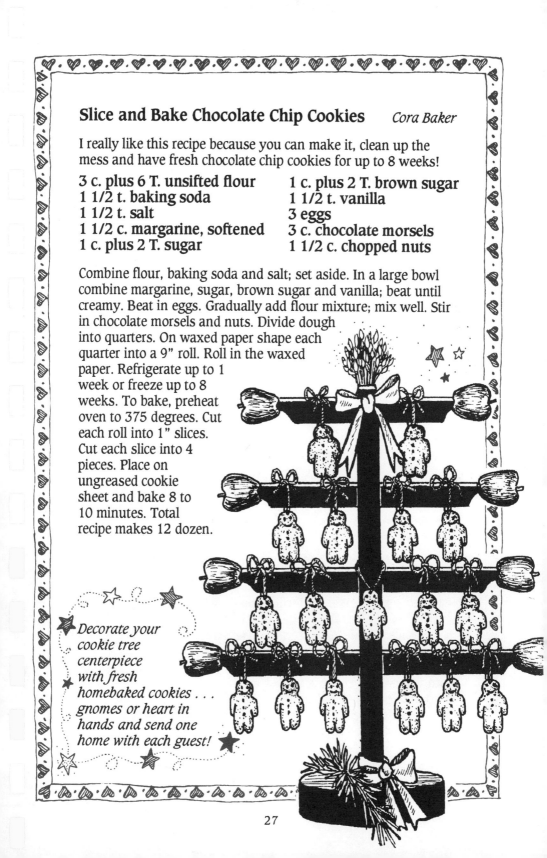

Slice and Bake Chocolate Chip Cookies *Cora Baker*

I really like this recipe because you can make it, clean up the mess and have fresh chocolate chip cookies for up to 8 weeks!

3 c. plus 6 T. unsifted flour
1 1/2 t. baking soda
1 1/2 t. salt
1 1/2 c. margarine, softened
1 c. plus 2 T. sugar

1 c. plus 2 T. brown sugar
1 1/2 t. vanilla
3 eggs
3 c. chocolate morsels
1 1/2 c. chopped nuts

Combine flour, baking soda and salt; set aside. In a large bowl combine margarine, sugar, brown sugar and vanilla; beat until creamy. Beat in eggs. Gradually add flour mixture; mix well. Stir in chocolate morsels and nuts. Divide dough into quarters. On waxed paper shape each quarter into a 9" roll. Roll in the waxed paper. Refrigerate up to 1 week or freeze up to 8 weeks. To bake, preheat oven to 375 degrees. Cut each roll into 1" slices. Cut each slice into 4 pieces. Place on ungreased cookie sheet and bake 8 to 10 minutes. Total recipe makes 12 dozen.

Decorate your cookie tree centerpiece with fresh homebaked cookies . . . gnomes or heart in hands and send one home with each guest!

Pumpkin Chocolate Chip Cookies

Cora Baker

4 c. flour	1 t. allspice
2 t. baking powder	2 t. nutmeg
2 t. cinnamon	1 t. salt

Combine the above ingredients and set aside.

1 lb. margarine	**2 T. vanilla**
2 eggs, beaten	**16 oz. can pumpkin**
2 c. sugar	**2 c. chocolate chips**

Cream the margarine and sugar together. Add eggs, vanilla and pumpkin. Stir in the dry ingredients. Stir in the chocolate chips. Drop by teaspoonsful onto ungreased baking sheets. Bake at 350 degrees for 15 minutes. Cool and ice with Chocolate Cream Cheese Frosting.

Chocolate Cream Cheese Frosting:

3 squares semi-sweet chocolate	**1/2 t. vanilla**
1 1/2 T. water	**1 1/4 c. powdered sugar**
3 oz. pkg. cream cheese, softened	

Microwave chocolate and water for 2 minutes on HIGH. Stir and cool to luke warm. Beat in cream cheese and vanilla. Beat in powdered sugar until smooth. Makes 1 1/4 cups.

★ ☆ ★

My daughter's class had an autumn picnic day and some of us moms were asked to provide an autumn treat. I had purchased a sunflower cookie cutter from Gooseberry Patch and decided to make sunflower cookies. I dyed the cookie dough with yellow food coloring and used mini chocolate chips as the seeds...the kids (and moms) loved them!

Lynn Peterson

White Chocolate Macadamia Nut Cookies

Cora Baker

3 c. flour
1 t. baking soda
1 t. salt
1 c. melted butter
2 c. white chocolate morsels, or small, white chocolate chunks
1 c. coarsely chopped macadamia nuts
3/4 c. sugar
3/4 c. packed brown sugar
1 t. vanilla
2 eggs

Combine flour, baking soda and salt; set aside. In a large bowl combine butter, sugars, vanilla and beat in eggs. Add flour, baking soda and salt. Stir in white chocolate chips and macadamia nuts. Chill dough. Drop by rounded teaspoonsful onto ungreased cookie sheet. Bake at 375 degrees for 8 to 10 minutes. Makes 100 cookies.

Old Fashioned Raisin Drop Cookies

Phyllis Peters

2 c. raisins
1 c. water
1 c. butter
1/2 t. cinnamon
1/2 t. nutmeg
1/2 c. nutmeats, chopped
4 c. flour
2 eggs, beaten
1 t. vanilla
1 t. baking powder
1 t. baking soda
1 3/4 c. white sugar
1/2 t. salt (optional)

Boil raisins in water until plump. Cool. Cream butter and sugar, add eggs and vanilla. Stir in raisins and water that remains on them. Gradually add rest of ingredients, stirring in nuts last, blend well. Drop by spoonful on ungreased baking sheet at desired size. Bake at 375 degrees for 12 to 15 minutes. Makes several dozen depending on size you make. These cookies freeze well.

To blanch almonds, place shelled nuts in a large bowl and cover with boiling water. Let stand 3 to 4 minutes before rinsing under cold water and slipping off skins.

Ernestine Hayes

Dinosaur Food

Sarah Arrington

These cookies are fun to make with kids. No hot oven, no waiting for the cookies to bake and they love the names of the ingredients!

1/4 c. dirt (cocoa)
1/2 c. swamp water (milk)
2 c. crushed bones (sugar)
1/2 c. fat (margarine)
3 1/2 c. grass (uncooked
    quick oats)

1/2 c. squashed bugs
    (crunchy peanut
    butter)
1 t. muddy water (vanilla)

Mix dirt, swamp water, crushed bones and fat. Bring to a boil; boil for one minute. Add grass, muddy water and squashed bugs. Stir until bugs dissolve. Drop on waxed paper, let cool.

Caramel Chews

Linda Zell

A treat to please tots to teens (and adults too)! This is a good recipe for a cookie tray as it adds a different shape, texture and flavor from the usual selections.

1 c. corn flakes
1 c. crispy rice cereal
1 c. flaked coconut

1 c. chopped nuts
36 vanilla caramels
3 T. cream

In a large bowl measure corn flakes, rice cereal, coconut and nuts. In a double boiler, over low heat, melt the caramels and cream. Pour caramel over cereal mixture; combine. With buttered hands, make small balls. Place on waxed paper to cool. Keep covered.

I collect cookie cutters and hang them on a wrought iron tree-shaped cup holder. It saves storage space and is perfect in my country kitchen.

Tamara Gruber

Colonial Spice Cookies

Jean Stokes

These cookies were a favorite treat for children in colonial days.

2 1/2 c. sifted all-purpose flour (sift before measuring)
2 t. baking soda
1/2 t. allspice
1/2 t. ground cinnamon
1/2 t. ground cloves
1/4 t. ground ginger

3/4 c. butter or margarine, softened
1 c. granulated sugar
1 large egg
1/4 c. light molasses
confectioner's sugar

Sift dry ingredients together over waxed paper. Set flour mixture aside. Mix butter, granulated sugar and egg until mixture is thoroughly blended and light and fluffy. Using a wooden spoon, beat in the flour mixture alternately with molasses, beginning and ending with the flour mixture. Beat after each addition. Cover dough and refrigerate for 1 hour. Preheat oven to 375 degrees. Using solid vegetable shortening, lightly grease two cookie sheets. Remove chilled dough from wrapping. With hands, form 3/4" diameter balls. Place balls 1" apart on prepared baking sheets. Bake one sheet at a time on center rack about 8 minutes or until lightly browned. Transfer cookies to cooking racks. While still warm, sprinkle confectioner's sugar on cookies. Makes about 5 dozen cookies.

★ ★ ★

To make cookies taste fresh again when they start to get stale, drop a fresh piece of bread into the cookie container overnight. By morning, the bread will be as hard as a rock and the cookies moist again. Of course, an easier way is to just put them on a plate and pop them in the microwave for a few seconds.

Wendy Lee Paffenroth

Linzer Tarts

Diane Lorelli

This recipe for Linzer Tarts is an old one. The children enjoy cutting the small holes in the tops before baking and everyone helps with the "putting together."

6 c. unsifted flour
1 c. shortening
4 sticks margarine
6 egg yolks
1 t. vanilla

1/2 t. salt
1 1/2 c. sugar
1/2 c. white wine
raspberry jam

Combine shortening, margarine, egg yolks, vanilla, sugar and white wine; mix well. Add flour and salt. Mixture makes a soft dough. Do not chill dough. Roll out to a 1/4" thickness. Cut with floured biscuit cutter. Place rounds on ungreased cookie sheet. On every other round, cut out a small circle in the middle (using a doughnut hole cutter) or a tiny heart. Bake at 350 degrees for 12 minutes. Let cool. To assemble, place solid round on counter top. Top with about 1 teaspoon raspberry jam, cover with cut-out top cookie. Sprinkle with powdered sugar. Yield: Approximately 50 cookies.

Grammie and Grampie are in Florida and we all missed them so much. We decided to make them a special batch of cookies. We rolled out our favorite sugar cookie dough, then had the kids put their (clean) hands on the dough. We traced their little hands with a plastic knife then baked the cookies. The kids had a great time decorating the cookies, and my parents were absolutely thrilled to get batches of the three different sized hands. My dad even polyurethaned one hand cookie from each grandchild, wrote their name and the date on it and hung them on their tree!

Cynthia Reda

Grandpa John's Chocolate Chip Cookies

Karen Spreng

My father was a pastry chef all his life. When he would come home from the bakery, occasionally he would bring these chocolate chip cookies home. They were wonderful. Now as a mother with two young daughters, I have searched for cookies like these, but never could find them. So one day I asked my dad if he knew where I could get cookies "like I remember", and he was able to produce a copy of his recipe. I was excited! Those cookies were a delightful memory of past times. But when I looked at the recipe it was for 57 dozen, because it was for the bakery. Needless to say, thanks to the age of calculators and an engineer for a husband, we were able to break down the recipe. My daughters were excited when I baked the cookies and they went on to name them "Grandpa John's Cookies". Now when I ask them what they want for their birthday treats at school, the answer is always the same. Also, every year at Christmas, Grandpa John comes over to teach the girls a new recipe and we all bake Christmas goodies together. The girls are learning many secret family recipes, but above all, are learning from their grandfather, truly a master baker.

1 1/2 c. packed light brown sugar
1 1/3 c. granulated sugar
1 1/2 t. salt
1 1/2 t. baking soda
1 c. butter
1 c. shortening
5 eggs
6 1/2 c. sifted cake flour
24 oz. semi-sweet chocolate morsels

Cream together sugars, salt, baking soda, butter and shortening; beat well. Add eggs, one at a time, beating well. Add flour, mixing well after each cup. Add chocolate morsels. Drop the dough using a small ice cream scoop into baking pans lined with baking papers. Bake at 360 degrees for 10 to 12 minutes. Cool 5 minutes in pans before removing to a cooling rack. Makes approximately 7 dozen.

I am going to tell you a story that I remember like it was yesterday. I can see myself snuggled up in the big blue chair, next to our fireplace with my teddy bear. My mother was always in the kitchen baking up a batch of my favorite cookies. Just thinking back reminds me of the day we made them together. It was just days before Christmas and my mother was preparing the dough to make her sugar cookies. She called to me, and I jumped out of the blue chair to help her. I just knew it was time to punch out the dough with the reindeer cookie cutter and to put a cinnamon candy dot on his nose. The kitchen was warm, bright and filled with the vanilla aroma of fresh baked cookies. We always had to stay in the kitchen and cut out the cookies on that table. That was the rule. But on that day I decided to scramble off into the dining room, squishing my small piece of dough on my mother's oak table (which we only used for special occasions) and pushed really hard with the cookie cutter. After I picked up the dough, I noticed some indentations in the wood. Boy, I knew I was in for it! With tears in my eyes, I showed my mother what I had done.

She was very understanding and she hugged and kissed me, and told me how much she loved me. We don't have that big blue chair anymore, but I still have that old oak table and every year my two children and I make our favorite cookies on it. Everyday as I walk past that table and see all the nicks, scratches, and last but not least, that cookie cutter shape, I think back and remember each special day that went along with them. "You can't take these things to heaven with you, so you might as well enjoy them now," as my mother says. As we all sit down to eat Christmas dinner at the same table she used to serve Christmas dinner on, she still smiles when she looks at all those marks. And I know deep down inside, her heart smiles with her as well.

Sharon Scurto

34

Grandma McElwee's
Raisin-Filled Cookies

Lara McElwee Green

This recipe is synonymous with gold in our family. Whenever my sisters and I visited our grandma we hoped to taste the rich, sweet raisin filling of her infamous raisin-filled cookies. These cookies were "moan and groan" good! When grandma died, the recipe became a mystery and was lost for a few years. The recipe was recently rediscovered and dozens of cookies have been made. When I married, I received my grandma's cookbook as a wedding gift and have enjoyed "recreating" other recipes, but treasure this one!

2 c. light brown sugar, packed
1/8 t. salt
1 c. shortening
    (use 1/2 butter and 1/2
    vegetable shortening)

1 t. baking soda
4 c. flour
2 t. vanilla
3 eggs

Cream sugar, salt and shortening. Beat in eggs and vanilla. Sift together dry ingredients. Add to creamed mixture.

Raisin Filling:

1 c. light brown sugar, packed
1 T. flour
1 c. chopped nuts (optional)

1 c. water
1 1/2 c. ground raisins
1 T. lemon juice

Mix sugar and flour. Stir in water slowly. Add nuts, raisins and lemon juice. Cook until slightly thickened. Cool. Take two rounds of unbaked dough (rolled and cut with a drinking glass) and put a spoonful of filling in the center of one cookie. Put the second round on top of the bottom one. Bake at 350 degrees for 12 to 15 minutes. Enjoy!

I like to use a cookie cutter when making pies. For instance, for the top crust of an apple pie, use an apple cookie cutter. Cut into the actual top crust, then after placing the crust on the pie, put the cut-out apple off center so as not to cover the opening completely.

Grace Wood

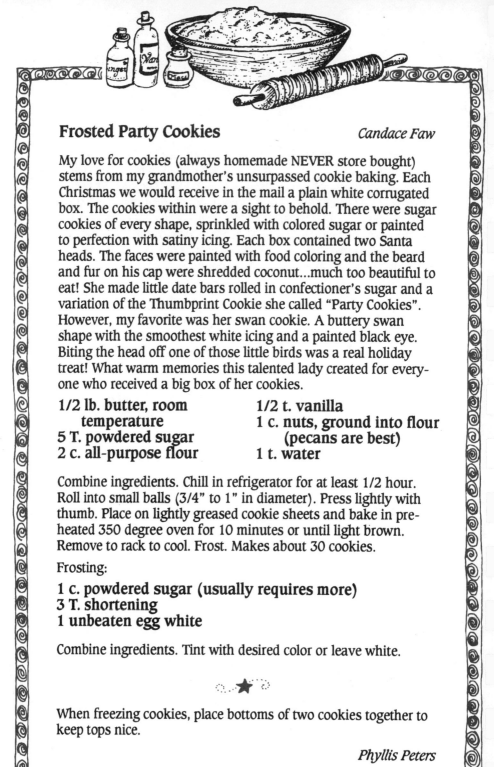

Frosted Party Cookies

Candace Faw

My love for cookies (always homemade NEVER store bought) stems from my grandmother's unsurpassed cookie baking. Each Christmas we would receive in the mail a plain white corrugated box. The cookies within were a sight to behold. There were sugar cookies of every shape, sprinkled with colored sugar or painted to perfection with satiny icing. Each box contained two Santa heads. The faces were painted with food coloring and the beard and fur on his cap were shredded coconut...much too beautiful to eat! She made little date bars rolled in confectioner's sugar and a variation of the Thumbprint Cookie she called "Party Cookies". However, my favorite was her swan cookie. A buttery swan shape with the smoothest white icing and a painted black eye. Biting the head off one of those little birds was a real holiday treat! What warm memories this talented lady created for everyone who received a big box of her cookies.

1/2 lb. butter, room temperature
5 T. powdered sugar
2 c. all-purpose flour

1/2 t. vanilla
1 c. nuts, ground into flour (pecans are best)
1 t. water

Combine ingredients. Chill in refrigerator for at least 1/2 hour. Roll into small balls (3/4" to 1" in diameter). Press lightly with thumb. Place on lightly greased cookie sheets and bake in preheated 350 degree oven for 10 minutes or until light brown. Remove to rack to cool. Frost. Makes about 30 cookies.

Frosting:

1 c. powdered sugar (usually requires more)
3 T. shortening
1 unbeaten egg white

Combine ingredients. Tint with desired color or leave white.

When freezing cookies, place bottoms of two cookies together to keep tops nice.

Phyllis Peters

White Velvet Cut-Outs

Sharon Hill

1 c. butter, softened
3 oz. cream cheese,
    softened
1 c. sugar

1 egg yolk
1/2 t. vanilla
2 1/2 c. flour
sprinkles or colored sugar

Cream butter and cream cheese together. Beat in sugar. Add egg yolk and vanilla, then stir in flour. Gather dough into a ball and chill overnight. To prepare, preheat oven to 350 degrees. On a lightly floured board, roll out dough to a 3/16" thickness. Cut into desired shapes. Place cookies on ungreased cookie sheets. Bake for 12 minutes or until edges are light brown. Cool on wire racks.

Glaze:

1 c. powdered sugar
1 T. water

1/2 t. lemon juice

Mix glaze ingredients together and spread a thin coat on each cookie, topping with colorful sprinkles or sugar. When glaze is dry, store cookies in an airtight container. Makes about 8 dozen.

Easy Colored Sugar

Lisa Sett

1/2 c. sugar
    (for each
    color desired)
1 drop liquid
    food coloring

Mix thoroughly until all sugar is colored. Store in airtight container. Use sugar for rolled sugar cookies or sprinkle over stencil onto cut-out cookies. Save extra topping for oatmeal!

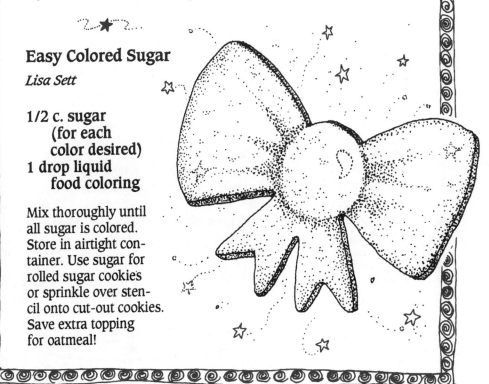

Brown Sugar Snappers

Kathy Hall

Great for kids to help with and they love the turtle shape!

6 T. butter or margarine	1/2 t. baking powder
1/3 c. shortening	1/2 t. baking soda
2/3 c. packed brown sugar	pecan halves
1/4 t. salt	large bag of candy coated
1 egg	milk chocolate candies
1 t. vanilla	16 oz. pkg. chocolate chips
1 3/4 c. flour	

Cream together butter or margarine, shortening and brown sugar until light and fluffy. Beat in egg and vanilla. Stir together flour, baking powder, baking soda and salt. Add to creamed mixture; mix well. Chill dough. On ungreased cookie sheet, arrange pecan halves in groups of 4 to form turtle feet. Roll dough into 1" balls. Press 3 or 4 candies into center of each ball, roll dough around candy. Place a ball atop each group of nuts. Bake in 325 degree preheated oven for 15 to 20 minutes. Meanwhile, melt chocolate chips. Remove cookies and cool for 2 minutes. Spread top of each cookie with some melted chocolate.

We have an annual "Cookie Swap" where everyone brings one batch of one type of Christmas cookie, along with the recipe; index cards (I save previous Christmas cards and write on the back of the picture side); and a pencil to copy the recipe. Everyone brings a tin or basket and circles a large table, taking three of every type of cookie until they are all gone. You leave with a batch of Christmas cookies, only now you have an assortment of homemade Christmas cookies to serve your own friends and relatives who drop by over the holidays. Tea, coffee and cake are served. With all the rushing of the season, we get to see each other for a few hours to chat, catch up, share photos and wish everyone a happy holiday.

Maureen Sanchirico

Pecan Sandies

Kathy Hall

1/2 c. butter
1/2 c. shortening
1 c. sugar
1 1/2 c. sifted flour
1/2 t. baking soda

1/2 t. baking powder
1/2 c. chopped pecans
white sugar or red &
   green sugar sprinkles
for Christmas

Preheat oven to 350 degrees. Cream butter and shortening; gradually add 1 cup sugar and cream again. Mix together dry ingredients; gradually add to creamed mixture. Stir in nuts. Chill 1/2 hour. Shape into 1" balls; place 2 inches apart on greased cookie sheet. Flatten balls to 1/3" with the bottom of a glass (slightly moisten the bottom) which has been dipped in white sugar or green/red sugar. Bake for 12 to 15 minutes.

Preacher's Cookies

Beverly Botten

Here is an easy, no-bake cookie recipe. We don't know the origin of the recipe or have an explanation of its unusual name, so we decided it was so named because you could start the cookies as the preacher arrived for a visit and be ready to serve them before he left your home!

2 c. sugar
1 stick butter or margarine
1/2 c. milk

1 t. vanilla
2 1/2 c. quick oatmeal
1/2 c. cocoa

In a 3-qt. saucepan bring the sugar, butter or margarine and milk to a boil. Stir occasionally to keep from scorching and boil for 3 to 4 minutes. Remove from heat and add the vanilla, oatmeal and cocoa. Stir well and drop by teaspoonsful on waxed paper. Allow to harden (15 to 30 minutes depending on the humidity) and then enjoy. Makes 48-60 cookies depending on the size of the cookie.

Holiday Poppy Seed Cookies

Deb Reinke

Here's our family's all-time favorite cookie recipe! My mother came across the recipe in a gas company cookbook in the 40's.

1 c. butter
1/2 c. sugar
1/4 t. salt
2 egg yolks
1 t. vanilla

2 c. sifted flour
3 T. poppy seeds
6 oz. semi-sweet
    chocolate chips, melted

Cream together butter, sugar and salt until well blended, light and fluffy. Add vanilla and egg yolks, one at at time; beat thoroughly. Stir in flour and blend well. Stir in poppy seeds. Shape dough into 1" balls. Place on ungreased cookie sheet 1" apart. Press in center of each cookie using the handle end of a wooden spoon. Bake at 375 degrees for 10 to 12 minutes. Remove from cookie sheet. Press center down again. When cold, fill centers with melted chocolate (using a baby's feeding spoon works great). Yield: 5 dozen.

✽ ★ ☆ ★ ✦

Over the years I have enjoyed using gingerbread people with names piped on them for place cards at parties during the Christmas season, as well as for Christmas Eve dinner. A word of warning, one year I decided to set the Christmas Eve dinner table early in the morning and put out the gingerbread people (I propped them against the wine glasses). To my horror, at about 4 o'clock they were all bent double, looking like they had stomach troubles. These guys need to be kept in a cool, dry place until placement. They add a lot of atmosphere and a wonderful fragrance to the table, and provide a nibble for those who just can't wait for everyone else to be served.

Christel Zuber Fishburn

Crispy Oatmeal Cookies

Doodles Young

1 c. butter or margarine, softened
1 c. sugar
1 c. lightly packed brown sugar
2 eggs
2 t. vanilla

1 1/2 c. flour
1 t. baking powder
1 t. baking soda
2 c. oatmeal
2 c. crispy rice cereal
1 c. coconut

Cream the butter and sugars. Add eggs and vanilla. Sift the flour, baking powder and soda; add to egg mixture. Add remaining ingredients and mix well. Drop by heaping teaspoonsful 2" apart on a greased baking sheet. Bake in a 350 degree oven for 10 minutes. Remove from baking sheet at once. Makes 5 to 6 dozen.

Farmhouse Chocolate Mint Cookies

Mary Murray

These cookies are great if you love mint-chocolate and they're always a hit at the annual Christmas cookie exchange.

3/4 c. (1 1/2 sticks) butter
1 1/2 c. firmly packed light brown sugar
2 T. water
12 oz. pkg. semi-sweet chocolate pieces
2 eggs

2 1/2 c. flour
1 1/4 t. baking soda
1/2 t. salt
1 lb. green chocolate mint wafers
chocolate sprinkles

Place butter, sugar, and water in saucepan on low heat until butter is melted. Add chocolate pieces and stir until partially melted. Remove from heat. Continue to stir until chocolate is completely melted. Pour into a large mixing bowl and let stand about 10 minutes to cool slightly. With mixer at high speed, beat in eggs one at a time. Reduce speed to low and add combined dry ingredients, beating just until blended. Chill dough about one hour. Heat oven to 350 degrees. Line 2 cookie sheets with foil. Take teaspoonsful of dough and roll into balls. Place 2" apart on cookie sheets. Bake 11 to 13 minutes (do not overbake). Immediately place mints on hot cookie. Allow to soften, then swirl mint over cookies and decorate with chocolate sprinkles. Remove from cookie sheet and cool completely.

Mary's Mother's Snowballs

Mary Murray

A cookie with a surprise...it's wrapped around a milk chocolate drop! I couldn't submit this without giving credit where credit is due, to my mother Donna Dye.

2 sticks butter, softened
2 c. finely chopped
   walnuts
3/4 c. sugar

8 oz. milk chocolate drops
2 c. flour, sifted
powdered sugar,
   for dusting

Cream butter and sugar well, until smooth. Add flour, then walnuts. Gather dough into disk-shape and wrap in plastic. Refrigerate at least 1/2 hour. Preheat oven to 350 degrees. Remove foil from candies and insert one inside a ball of dough 1" in diameter. Make sure each candy is completely covered by dough. Bake on ungreased baking sheet for about 12 minutes, until just baked through. Sift over powdered sugar while still warm.

I'm a teacher and I make dough ornaments with my students for every holiday or "theme" weeks. We'll be making mittens out of dough again this year. We make two ornaments for each child, one with their name, the other with the year. The kids love them!

Angie Yanchik

When I was PTO President, I baked heart in hand cutout cookies. The cookies made great "thank-you's" to the volunteers with a note included saying, "Thank you for being there to lend a helping hand."

Carol Jones

42

Two-Tone Icebox Cookies

Mary Murray

2 sticks (8 oz.) butter,
   softened to room
   temperature
1 c. sugar
1 egg plus 1 egg yolk

1 t. vanilla extract
2 3/4 c. flour
2 T. unsweetened cocoa
   powder
1 egg white, beaten

In a large bowl, cream the butter and sugar. Beat in the egg and egg yolk, then beat in the vanilla. Gradually add the flour. Divide the dough into two equal portions. Beat the cocoa into one portion. Form the dough into two balls. Follow directions for shaping cookies into pinwheels, checkerboards or bulls-eyes. Wrap dough in plastic wrap and refrigerate for at least 4 hours. Cut into 1/4" slices. Preheat oven to 350 degrees and lightly grease a baking sheet. Space cookies 1" apart and bake for 8 to 10 minutes.

Checkerboard:
Divide the dough into alternate ropes of light and dark. Working with 4 ropes (2 of each color), press a light dough rope and a dark dough rope together. Repeat with the other ropes. Place one pair of ropes on top of the other, alternating light and dark doughs. Press the ropes together to form a long roll, repeat with remaining dough. Wrap each roll in plastic wrap and refrigerate 4 hours to firm. When you're ready to bake, just slice to 1/4" and bake 8 to 10 minutes at 350 degrees on a lightly greased cookie sheet.

Bull's Eyes:
Wrap a dough rectangle of one color around a dough log of another color. It's fun to make half the cookies with dark dough centers, the other half with light dough centers. Follow the same directions as above for refrigerating dough and baking.

Pinwheel:
To make these, layer two rectangles of different colored doughs together, then roll them up in a log shape and slice. Follow the same directions as above for refrigerating and baking.

Log Cookies:
Roll dough into 1/2" thick ropes and cut into 2" lengths. Dip each log into beaten egg white, then into chopped or sliced almond.

PURE VANILLA

Clove Cookies

Ernestine Hayes

Delicious with hot tea in the winter and lemonade in the summer!

1/2 c. butter	1 egg
1 c. sugar	1 c. all-purpose flour
1 t. vanilla	1 t. ground cloves

Melt butter in a small pan over medium heat. Remove from heat and stir in sugar until well combined; then stir in vanilla. Add egg and beat until mixture is smooth. In a small bowl stir together flour and cloves; gradually add to butter mixture, blending thoroughly. Drop dough by level teaspoonsful onto well-greased baking sheets, spacing cookies 2 1/2" to 3" apart. Bake at 350 degrees for 12 to 14 minutes or until edges are golden brown and puffy tops start to crinkle and collapse. Immediately transfer cookies to racks and let cool. Store in airtight containers. Makes about 4 dozen crisp, buttery morsels.

Mud Cookies

Cathrin Owens

My grandma Hazel and I used to love making mud cookies together. The memories just flood back when I whip up a batch of these tasty treats!

2 c. sugar	1/4 c. peanut butter
1/2 c. milk	3 c. oatmeal
1/2 c. cocoa	1 c. chopped walnuts
1/2 c. butter	

Mix sugar, milk, cocoa and butter and boil for one minute. Remove from heat and add peanut butter, oatmeal and walnuts; mixing well. Drop on waxed paper.

★ ✩✦

Use smaller cutters to decorate frosted cookies. Just press cutter lightly into the soft icing and make a slight imprint. Children seem to enjoy this extra touch. I know some "big kids" that are equally delighted in choosing the cookie with their favorite imprint too!

Judy Hand

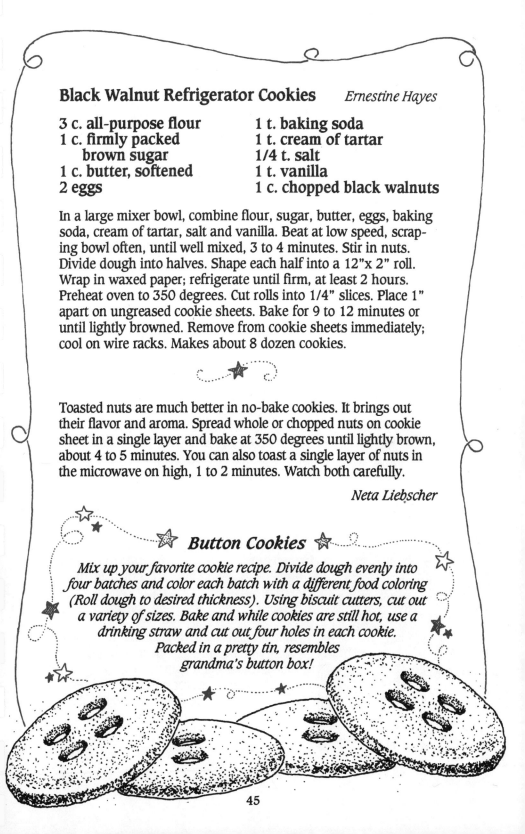

Black Walnut Refrigerator Cookies *Ernestine Hayes*

3 c. all-purpose flour
1 c. firmly packed
   brown sugar
1 c. butter, softened
2 eggs

1 t. baking soda
1 t. cream of tartar
1/4 t. salt
1 t. vanilla
1 c. chopped black walnuts

In a large mixer bowl, combine flour, sugar, butter, eggs, baking soda, cream of tartar, salt and vanilla. Beat at low speed, scraping bowl often, until well mixed, 3 to 4 minutes. Stir in nuts. Divide dough into halves. Shape each half into a 12"x 2" roll. Wrap in waxed paper; refrigerate until firm, at least 2 hours. Preheat oven to 350 degrees. Cut rolls into 1/4" slices. Place 1" apart on ungreased cookie sheets. Bake for 9 to 12 minutes or until lightly browned. Remove from cookie sheets immediately; cool on wire racks. Makes about 8 dozen cookies.

Toasted nuts are much better in no-bake cookies. It brings out their flavor and aroma. Spread whole or chopped nuts on cookie sheet in a single layer and bake at 350 degrees until lightly brown, about 4 to 5 minutes. You can also toast a single layer of nuts in the microwave on high, 1 to 2 minutes. Watch both carefully.

Neta Liebscher

☆ *Button Cookies* ☆

Mix up your favorite cookie recipe. Divide dough evenly into four batches and color each batch with a different food coloring (Roll dough to desired thickness). Using biscuit cutters, cut out a variety of sizes. Bake and while cookies are still hot, use a drinking straw and cut out four holes in each cookie.
Packed in a pretty tin, resembles
grandma's button box!

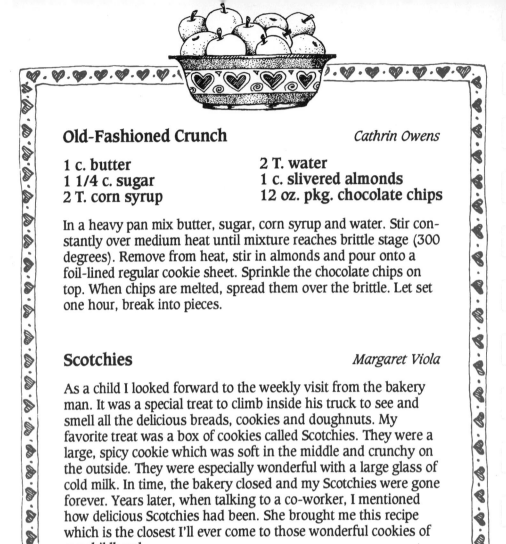

Old-Fashioned Crunch

Cathrin Owens

1 c. butter
1 1/4 c. sugar
2 T. corn syrup

2 T. water
1 c. slivered almonds
12 oz. pkg. chocolate chips

In a heavy pan mix butter, sugar, corn syrup and water. Stir constantly over medium heat until mixture reaches brittle stage (300 degrees). Remove from heat, stir in almonds and pour onto a foil-lined regular cookie sheet. Sprinkle the chocolate chips on top. When chips are melted, spread them over the brittle. Let set one hour, break into pieces.

Scotchies

Margaret Viola

As a child I looked forward to the weekly visit from the bakery man. It was a special treat to climb inside his truck to see and smell all the delicious breads, cookies and doughnuts. My favorite treat was a box of cookies called Scotchies. They were a large, spicy cookie which was soft in the middle and crunchy on the outside. They were especially wonderful with a large glass of cold milk. In time, the bakery closed and my Scotchies were gone forever. Years later, when talking to a co-worker, I mentioned how delicious Scotchies had been. She brought me this recipe which is the closest I'll ever come to those wonderful cookies of my childhood.

3/4 c. shortening
1 c. sugar
1 egg
1/4 c. molasses
2 c. flour

1/2 t. salt
3 t. baking soda
1 t. cinnamon
1 t. cloves
1 t. ginger

Mix shortening, sugar, egg and molasses. Add dry ingredients. Shape into quarter-sized balls and flatten with a jar. Bake at 350 degrees for 8 minutes. Remove from oven while still light colored and puffed up.

Apricot-Filled Cookies

Charmaine Hahl

Cookie Dough:

1 c. sifted flour	1 c. quick-cooking oatmeal
1/2 t. baking soda	1/2 c. melted butter
1/4 t. salt	2/3 c. brown sugar

Filling:

1/4 c. nuts	1/2 c. water
1/2 c. dried apricots	1/2 c. sugar

Heat oven to 350 degrees. Grease 8" pan. Blender-chop nuts, empty into a small mixing bowl. Put apricots and water into blender, cover and process at LIQUIFY until smooth. Stop and push ingredients down to blades. Add sugar and process at LIQUIFY until smooth. Pour over nuts and mix well. Sift flour, baking soda and salt into large mixing bowl, add oatmeal. Put butter and brown sugar into blender. Cover and process at MIX until smooth. Add to flour mixture and mix well. Spread 2/3 of dough evenly in the prepared pan, top with apricot filling, top with remaining dough. Pack down lightly. Bake for 30 to 35 minutes. Cool before cutting into bars. Yield: 32 bars.

★ ☆ ★

Every year I try to come up with a different idea for our cookie table or craft table for our church bazaar. This year I have fallen in love with your Christmas moose cookie cutter. Living in the upper peninsula of Michigan, we have the "real" thing roaming around in the wild. This year I shall make molasses "Christmoose" cookies for our bazaar!

Judy Jones

To help your food gifts get safely through the mail, you may want to use zip lock bags, leaving air in, and packing with newspaper in a sturdy box. Also bubble wrap (the larger the bubbles the better), popcorn or "environmentally friendly" polystyrene peanuts are excellent choices for packaging. Be sure to mark the box, "Perishable Food, Open at Once."

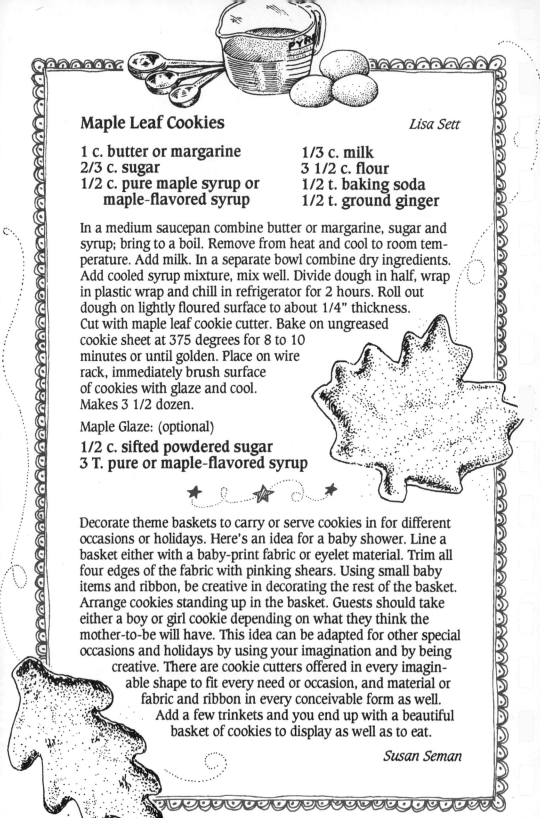

Maple Leaf Cookies

Lisa Sett

1 c. butter or margarine
2/3 c. sugar
1/2 c. pure maple syrup or
   maple-flavored syrup

1/3 c. milk
3 1/2 c. flour
1/2 t. baking soda
1/2 t. ground ginger

In a medium saucepan combine butter or margarine, sugar and syrup; bring to a boil. Remove from heat and cool to room temperature. Add milk. In a separate bowl combine dry ingredients. Add cooled syrup mixture, mix well. Divide dough in half, wrap in plastic wrap and chill in refrigerator for 2 hours. Roll out dough on lightly floured surface to about 1/4" thickness. Cut with maple leaf cookie cutter. Bake on ungreased cookie sheet at 375 degrees for 8 to 10 minutes or until golden. Place on wire rack, immediately brush surface of cookies with glaze and cool. Makes 3 1/2 dozen.

Maple Glaze: (optional)
1/2 c. sifted powdered sugar
3 T. pure or maple-flavored syrup

Decorate theme baskets to carry or serve cookies in for different occasions or holidays. Here's an idea for a baby shower. Line a basket either with a baby-print fabric or eyelet material. Trim all four edges of the fabric with pinking shears. Using small baby items and ribbon, be creative in decorating the rest of the basket. Arrange cookies standing up in the basket. Guests should take either a boy or girl cookie depending on what they think the mother-to-be will have. This idea can be adapted for other special occasions and holidays by using your imagination and by being creative. There are cookie cutters offered in every imaginable shape to fit every need or occasion, and material or fabric and ribbon in every conceivable form as well. Add a few trinkets and you end up with a beautiful basket of cookies to display as well as to eat.

Susan Seman

Zucchini Peanut Butter Cookies   *Mary Dungan*

1 1/2 c. all-purpose flour
1/2 c. crunchy
   peanut butter
1 c. grated unpeeled
   zucchini
1/2 c. packed brown sugar
1/2 c. granulated sugar

1 t. baking soda
1/2 c. margarine
1 egg, beaten
1 t. vanilla
1 c. chopped roasted
   peanuts
1/2 c. chocolate bits

Cut peanut butter into flour. In another bowl, thoroughly combine zucchini, baking soda, margarine and sugars. Add egg. Combine with flour mixture, add vanilla. Stir in nuts (I have used pecans in place of peanuts and also hickory nuts) and chocolate bits. Chill dough at least 2 hours. Drop by teaspoonsful onto greased baking sheet. Bake at 375 degrees for 12 to 15 minutes. Let cool. Yield: about 6 dozen cookies.

Salted Peanut Chews   *Neta Liebscher*

1 1/2 c. flour
1/2 c. brown sugar
3/4 c. butter, divided in half
3 c. miniature marshmallows
2 c. peanut butter-flavored
   baking chips

2/3 c. light corn syrup
2 t. vanilla
2 c. crisp rice cereal
2 c. salted peanuts

Combine flour, brown sugar and 1/2 of butter; mix well. Press into a 13"x9" ungreased pan. Bake at 350 degrees for 12 to 15 minutes until lightly brown. Top with marshmallows and bake 3 to 5 minutes until marshmallows begin to melt. Set aside. In a large pan cook and stir peanut butter chips, corn syrup, vanilla and remaining butter until melted and smooth. Remove from heat and stir in cereal and peanuts. Pour over crust and marshmallows until all is covered. Cool; cut into 2"x2" squares or smaller. Yield: 30 to 36 squares.

Grammy's Sugar Cookie Recipe
Sharon Scurto

3/4 c. butter
1 c. sugar
2 eggs
1 t. vanilla

2 1/2 c. all-purpose flour
1 t. baking powder
1 t. salt

Mix thoroughly butter, sugar, eggs and vanilla. Blend in flour, baking powder and salt. Cover, chill at least 1 hour. Heat oven to 400 degrees. Roll dough 1/8" thick on lightly floured, cloth-covered board. Cut into desired shapes with metal cookie cutters. Place on baking sheet. Bake 6 to 8 minutes or until very light brown. Sprinkle with colored sugar, jimmies or cinnamon dot candies. A cookie paint may also be applied before baking. Makes about 4 dozen cookies.

Cookie Paint:

If you choose to paint your cookies, make sure not to sprinkle cookies with sugar. Before baking, paint designs on cookies with small paintbrushes using cookie paint. Divide small amounts of evaporated milk (or mixture of 1 egg yolk and 1/4 teaspoon water) among several cups. Color each with a different food color. If paint thickens, add a few drops of water.

★ ✿★✿ ★

Buy cookie cutters that can go with a song or story. My children and I really enjoy singing songs as we eat cookies. For instance, farm animals for "Old MacDonald Had a Farm"; a dog for "Bingo"; and a teapot for "I'm a Little Teapot". Best of all a candle cookie cutter can be used for "This Little Light of Mine."

Rachel Gossett

If cookies don't taste as yummy as they should, melt chocolate chips and butter together until the right consistency for dipping. Dip one-half of the cookie in the chocolate mixture.

Cyndi Guemmer

Chocolate Dipped Butter Cookies
Donna Kincaid

2 1/3 c. flour
1/4 t. salt
1 c. butter, softened
2/3 c. sugar

1 egg yolk
1 t. vanilla
1 c. finely chopped nuts

In a large bowl, with electric mixer at medium speed, beat butter, sugar, egg yolk and vanilla until light and fluffy. Gradually stir in flour, salt and nuts, until well blended. With hands shape dough into two rolls 1 1/2" in diameter. Wrap in foil or plastic wrap. Refrigerate until firm, about 2 hours. Preheat oven to 350 degrees. Lightly grease cookie sheets. With sharp knife, cut into slices 1/4" thick. Place cookies 1" apart on cookie sheets. Bake 8 to 10 minutes, until lightly browned. Remove and cool. Make chocolate dip.

Chocolate Dip:

6 oz. pkg. semi-sweet
   chocolate pieces
3 T. butter
1 T. hot water

In a small saucepan, over low heat, melt chocolate and butter; add hot water. Dip half of each cookie into chocolate mixture. Sprinkle with chopped nuts, chocolate jimmies or nonpareils.

Cinnamon Sticks
Martha Terrell

1 c. all-purpose flour
1 c. sugar
2 t. cinnamon
1 1/2 sticks butter or
   margarine

1 egg, separated
1/2 t. vanilla
1 c. pecans, finely chopped

Sift together flour, sugar and cinnamon. Cream butter, then work into flour mixture. Add egg yolk and vanilla; mix well. Spread to 1/4" thickness on lightly greased jelly roll pan. Brush egg white on with pastry brush. Sprinkle liberally with pecans. Bake at 325 degrees for 30 minutes, or until lightly brown. Cut into rectangles. Remove to wire rack to cool. Delicious!

Night Before Christmas Mice

Martha Terrell

For a special gift, include a copy of **The Night Before Christmas** and flavored hot cocoa mix!

3/4 c. sugar
1/2 c. softened butter
   or margarine
1/2 c. shortening
1 t. vanilla
1 egg
2 1/4 c. all-purpose flour

1/4 c. unsweetened cocoa
1/2 t. baking powder
mini semi-sweet baking
   chips
red or black string licorice
   cut into 2" pieces or
   colored curling ribbon

Heat oven to 325 degrees. Beat sugar, butter and shortening until fluffy. Add vanilla and egg; blend well. Lightly spoon flour into measuring cup and level off. Stir in flour, cocoa and baking powder; mixing well. Shape dough into 1" balls. To form mouse, pinch one end of ball to form nose. Make two tiny balls of dough and flatten slightly for ears. Gently press into dough on upper front of each mouse. Press 2 mini chocolate chips into dough below ears, for eyes. Place 2" apart on ungreased cookie sheet. Bake 8 to 10 minutes or until set. Immediately press licorice or curling ribbon into the mouse for a tail. Remove and cool on waxed paper. Make 3 dozen mice. Adorable!

The Christmas bulb cookie cutter is a great gift for someone special. Make several cookies, frost them in bright colors, put a small hole in the base of the bulb (prior to baking), string the bulbs with string licorice, knot the licorice between the bulbs and add a note saying, "You light up my life."

Carol Jones

Oatmeal Country Hermits

Judy Hand

2 c. quick or old-fashioned
   oats, uncooked
1 1/2 c. sifted flour
1 c. melted butter
1 c. packed brown sugar
3/4 c. raisins
1/2 c. chopped nuts

1 egg
1/4 c. milk
1 t. cinnamon
1 t. vanilla
3/4 t. salt
1/2 t. baking soda
1/4 t. nutmeg

Preheat oven to 350 degrees. In a large bowl combine all ingredients; mix well. Drop batter by rounded teaspoons onto a foil-lined cookie sheet. Bake 8 to 10 minutes or until lightly brown. Cool for 1 minute on cookie sheet; remove to wire cooling rack. Store in tightly covered container. Makes 3 1/2 delicious dozen.

★☆ ☆★☆ ★

Rudolph Cookies

Use your favorite sugar cookie recipe or gingerbread cookie recipe to make Rudolph cookies. A gingerbread man cutter is needed. Turn the cookie upside down as if he is standing on his head. The head will be the head for Rudolph, the arms are his ears, and legs are his antlers. Use frosting to make the eyes and a big red nose. Decorate the antlers with lines of white icing. Place two green holly leaves above the eyes and a red bow on top to finish him off for the holiday. These cookies are fun for the kids to make. You could use a round jellied candy for the nose. Be creative!

Chris Montgomery

Many cookies that require rolling out can instead be formed into rolls, then wrapped in waxed paper and chilled, or wrapped in plastic wrap or foil and frozen. When needed, slice cookies 1/8" to 1/4" thick, place on cookie sheet and bake according to directions.

Tamara Gruber

Coffee Bars

Katherine Gaughan

1/2 c. shortening
1 c. brown sugar
1 egg
1/2 c. STRONG hot coffee
1 2/3 c. flour
1/2 t. baking powder

1/2 t. baking soda
1/2 t. cinnamon
1/2 t. salt
1/2 c. raisins
1/4 c. chopped walnuts

Combine in order, the shortening, sugar, egg, coffee, flour, baking powder, baking soda, cinnamon, salt, raisins and walnuts. Spread into a greased jelly roll pan. Bake at 350 degrees for 15 minutes. Cool in pan.

Icing:

1 1/2 c. powdered sugar
1 T. butter, softened

1 t. vanilla
3 T. hot coffee

Combine ingredients and spread onto cooled bars. Let icing set and then cut into bars or diamonds. Great for teas.

Crispy Chocolate Chip Cookies

Pat Akers

2 sticks margarine
1 c. oil
1 c. brown sugar
1 c. granulated sugar
1 egg
1 t. coconut flavoring
1 t. butter flavoring
2 t. vanilla

3 1/2 c. flour
1 t. cream of tartar
1/2 t. salt
1 t. baking soda
1 c. quick oats
1 c. crispy rice cereal
1 c. flaked coconut
1 c. chocolate chips

Cream margarine, sugar, egg and oil. Add flavorings. Stir cream of tartar, salt and baking soda into flour. Add to creamed mixture, then all other dry ingredients. Drop onto ungreased cookie sheet by teaspoonsful. Bake at 350 degrees for 10 to 12 minutes.

Carrot Chip Cookies

Pat Akers

1 1/2 c. all-purpose flour
1 1/4 t. ground cinnamon
3/4 t. baking soda
1/2 t. ground nutmeg
1/2 c. butter
1/3 c. packed light
    brown sugar

1/2 c. granulated sugar
1 large egg
3/4 c. coarsely grated
    carrots
1/2 c. walnuts
2/3 c. white chocolate
    chips

Heat oven to 350 degrees. Mix flour, cinnamon, baking soda and nutmeg. Cream butter, sugars and egg in a large bowl. With mixer on low speed, blend carrots, then flour mixture. Beat just until blended. Stir in nuts and chips. Drop by rounded tea-spoonsful on ungreased cookie sheets. Bake for 12 to 14 minutes, until edges are lightly browned and crispy. Tops will be soft to the touch. Cool slightly on sheets, then transfer to racks to finish cooling...that is if you can keep everyone from eating them while they are still warm!

A great gift for any child is a basket full of cookie cutters, sprinkles, a child size apron that you can decorate with their name, a rolling pin, recipes for cut-out cookies and a simple icing. For starters you could add refrigerated dough found at the supermarket.

Cathrin Owens

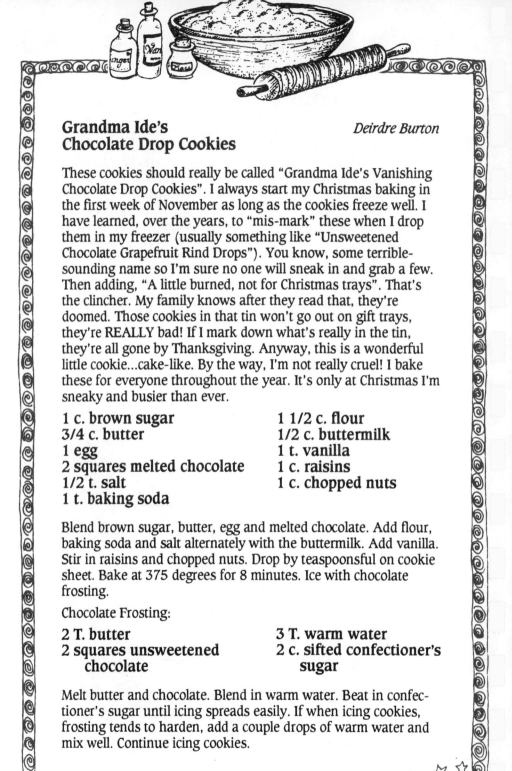

Grandma Ide's Chocolate Drop Cookies

Deirdre Burton

These cookies should really be called "Grandma Ide's Vanishing Chocolate Drop Cookies". I always start my Christmas baking in the first week of November as long as the cookies freeze well. I have learned, over the years, to "mis-mark" these when I drop them in my freezer (usually something like "Unsweetened Chocolate Grapefruit Rind Drops"). You know, some terrible-sounding name so I'm sure no one will sneak in and grab a few. Then adding, "A little burned, not for Christmas trays". That's the clincher. My family knows after they read that, they're doomed. Those cookies in that tin won't go out on gift trays, they're REALLY bad! If I mark down what's really in the tin, they're all gone by Thanksgiving. Anyway, this is a wonderful little cookie...cake-like. By the way, I'm not really cruel! I bake these for everyone throughout the year. It's only at Christmas I'm sneaky and busier than ever.

1 c. brown sugar	1 1/2 c. flour
3/4 c. butter	1/2 c. buttermilk
1 egg	1 t. vanilla
2 squares melted chocolate	1 c. raisins
1/2 t. salt	1 c. chopped nuts
1 t. baking soda	

Blend brown sugar, butter, egg and melted chocolate. Add flour, baking soda and salt alternately with the buttermilk. Add vanilla. Stir in raisins and chopped nuts. Drop by teaspoonsful on cookie sheet. Bake at 375 degrees for 8 minutes. Ice with chocolate frosting.

Chocolate Frosting:

2 T. butter	3 T. warm water
2 squares unsweetened chocolate	2 c. sifted confectioner's sugar

Melt butter and chocolate. Blend in warm water. Beat in confectioner's sugar until icing spreads easily. If when icing cookies, frosting tends to harden, add a couple drops of warm water and mix well. Continue icing cookies.

Caramel Candy Bars

Jennifer Broski

14 oz. pkg. caramel candies
1/3 c. milk
2 c. flour
2 c. quick-cooking or
    regular oats
1 1/2 c. packed brown sugar
1 t. baking soda

1/2 t. salt
1 egg
1 c. margarine, softened
6 oz. pkg. semi-sweet
    chocolate chips
1 c. chopped walnuts or
    dry roasted peanuts

Heat oven to 350 degrees. Grease rectangular pan (13"x9"x2").
Heat candies and milk in a 2 qt. saucepan over low heat, stirring
frequently until smooth; remove from heat. Mix flour, oats,
brown sugar, baking soda, salt and egg in a large bowl. Stir in
margarine with fork until mixture is crumbly. Press half of the
crumbly mixture in pan. Bake for 10 minutes. Sprinkle with
chocolate chips and walnuts; drizzle with caramel mixture.
Sprinkle remaining crumbly mixture over top. Bake until golden
brown, 20 to 25 minutes. Cool for 30 minutes. Loosen edges
from sides of pan, cool completely. Cut into bars about 2"x1".
Makes 54 cookies.

★ ☆ ★

Spend one day getting out all your favorite recipes (and some
new ones) with all the ingredients and measuring cups, spoons,
bowls, etc. needed for mixing. Spend that one day mixing up
many kinds of cookie dough to be refrigerated. No cooking
today! Within the next few days, all you
have to do is bake cookies, cool them
and pack for storing in tins to be
put on shelf, or in the freezer to
save for eating and giving. This
simple plan will make cookie
baking more fun and less work.

Gwen Mansini

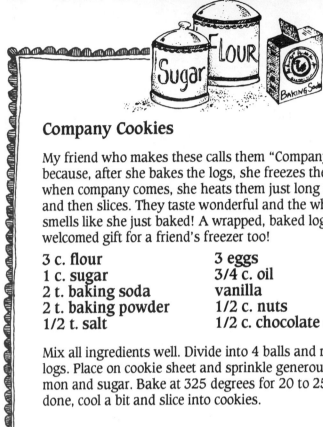

Company Cookies

Diane Dollak

My friend who makes these calls them "Company Cookies" because, after she bakes the logs, she freezes them and then when company comes, she heats them just long enough to thaw and then slices. They taste wonderful and the whole house smells like she just baked! A wrapped, baked log or two makes a welcomed gift for a friend's freezer too!

3 c. flour	3 eggs
1 c. sugar	3/4 c. oil
2 t. baking soda	vanilla
2 t. baking powder	1/2 c. nuts
1/2 t. salt	1/2 c. chocolate chips (or more)

Mix all ingredients well. Divide into 4 balls and roll into long logs. Place on cookie sheet and sprinkle generously with cinnamon and sugar. Bake at 325 degrees for 20 to 25 minutes. When done, cool a bit and slice into cookies.

Chocolate Cut-Out Cookies

Elenna Firme
Gooseberry Patch Artisan

2/3 c. shortening	2 pkg. unsweetened chocolate
1 1/2 c. sugar	(same as 2 squares melted)
2 eggs	4 c. flour
1 t. vanilla	2 1/2 t. baking powder
4 T. milk	1/2 t. salt

Cream shortening and sugar. Add eggs, vanilla and milk. Blend in chocolate and beat well. Add sifted dry ingredients and mix thoroughly. Roll out on floured surface about 1/4" thick and cut with cookie cutters. Bake at 375 degrees until done. Do not overbake chocolate cookies.

Always dip cookie cutter in flour to minimize sticking.

Michele Urdahl

Grandma's Sand Tarts

Katherine Gaughan

Although the dough is a bear to work with, the results are well worth the effort. For me and my family Sand Tarts are the best Christmas cookie!

4 sticks butter (1 lb.), well softened
4 c. powdered sugar

4 c. flour
4 eggs
1 t. vanilla

Combine in order...butter, sugar, eggs, vanilla and flour. Chill thoroughly, at least overnight. Use only small amounts of dough at a time. Leave remaining dough in freezer. Keeping hands and board well floured, roll out dough very thin. Cut into desired shapes. Sprinkle with colored sugar, jimmies or cinnamon/sugar. Bake in a 375 degree preheated oven on ungreased cookie sheets 6 to 8 minutes or until edges just begin to turn golden. Watch carefully. Quantity depends on shape size. Hint: You can make your own sugar sprinkles by mixing sugar and food coloring in a zippered food bag. Place sugar into a bowl and leave out overnight so that the sugar granulates again. You can make a large variety of colors and shades and the color doesn't fade when you bake.

My first cookie cutter was given to me by my aunt when I was 12 years old, first learning to bake. She sent me a little gingerbread man cookie cutter with the gingerbread recipe card and a little poem with words of encouragement. From that day on, it was included as a sort of fun family tradition. On special occasions like birthdays, Christmas or important family events, we send a cookie cutter, cookie recipe and some- times even a sample.

Kathy Jean Milligan

In the cookie of life, friends are the chocolate chips.

59

Herb Gardner's Chocolate-Mint Sand Tarts

Judy Hand

2 sticks butter, melted
2 c. flour
3 t. chocolate chips (I usually use the mini chips)
2 t. almond flavoring
3 t. dried spearmint

Mix all the ingredients in a large bowl. Roll mixture into small balls, place on ungreased cookie sheet and press with thumb. Bake at 350 degrees for 10 to 12 minutes. Cool and dust with powdered sugar. Makes 5 dozen small sand tarts. Hint: For a sweeter tart, 3 teaspoons of sugar may be added to mixture.

Cookie Cutter Pins

Here's an idea for using the mini tin cookie cutters offered in the Gooseberry Patch catalog.

Supplies:

1 x-acto knife
2 oz. white sculptor's clay
(the kind you can bake)

clear acrylic spray
mini tin cookie cutters
pin backs

Remove blade from knife. The handle will serve as your rolling pin. Roll out small balls of clay onto a non-metal surface (I use the back of a casserole dish). Press cutter onto clay and carefully remove excess. Continue in this manner until surface is full. Bake at 275 degrees for 15 minutes. Let cool. Paint with acrylic paints mixed with a drop or two of water for a more sheer effect. Glue on the pin backs. You can also make mini ornaments by making a small hole at the top of the cut-out before baking. An extra thin ribbon can then be used to hang your ornament. After painting, spray with a clear acrylic spray to keep paint from rubbing off. These make nice little gifts or bazaar crafts and are budget friendly! 2 oz. clay yields approximately 38 pins.

Connie Fannin

Chocolate Bittersweets

Sandra Laufer

1/2 c. butter	1 t. vanilla
1/2 c. powdered sugar	1 to 1 1/4 c. flour
1/4 t. salt	

Cream butter, sugar, salt and vanilla. Gradually add flour. Shape into balls, using 1/2 teaspoon of dough for each. Place on ungreased cookie sheet. Press hole in center with finger. Bake at 350 degrees for 12 to 15 minutes, until delicately browned on edges. Fill while still warm and frost.

Creamy Nut Filling:

3 oz. pkg. cream cheese	2 T. flour
1 c. powdered sugar	1/2 c. nuts
vanilla	1/2 c. flaked coconut

Soften cream cheese. Blend in sugar, flour and vanilla; cream well. Stir in nuts and coconut.

Frosting:

1/2 c. chocolate chips	2 T. butter
2 T. water	1/2 c. powdered sugar

Cook chips, water and butter in a small pan, stirring occasionally, until melted. Remove from heat, add sugar and beat until smooth.

★ ☆ ★

If you're in a hurry to frost your cookies, you can take a few chocolate chips and place them on hot cookies. When they begin to melt, spread the chocolate over the entire cookie top. Sprinkle with colored sprinkles.

Sharon Scurto

It's fun and so easy to stencil your windows with a variety of holiday designs. Trace cookie cutter shapes onto a big sheet of construction paper, cut out designs and tape sheet (with cut out designs) onto your window, gently spraying with Christmas snow.

Bird Nest Clusters

Kimberley Bercaw

This recipe became an Easter favorite of our family's, using jelly beans as "eggs" in the nests. We've improvised over the years by experimenting with different garnishes for different holidays, and now they are a favorite year round. Your "eggs" can be candy conversation hearts for Valentine's Day; green and white hearts for St. Patrick's Day; candy corn for Halloween...the possibilities are endless!

6 oz. pkg. semi-sweet chocolate chips
1/2 c. peanut butter
4 c. chow mein noodles

Melt the chocolate chips and peanut butter in a double boiler, or in a glass bowl in the microwave, for approximately one minute. Remove the mixture from the double boiler or microwave and stir until well mixed. Add the chow mein noodles tossing slightly to coat evenly. Drop golf ball-sized clusters on cookie sheet covered with waxed paper. Fill the birds nests with your favorite "holiday" garnish before they cool. Makes about 2 dozen bird nests.

Every year for my daughters' birthdays, I give each of them a cookie cutter. It may be old or new, tied in with the birthday theme or not, but is special in one way or another. They each have a tin to keep their cookie cutters in and, someday, when they move away from home, they'll have their own set of cookie cutters to use when making cookies. This idea could be extended to Christmas by attaching a cookie cutter with a ribbon to presents.

Suzanne Carbaugh

Taffy Apple Cookies

Kathy Wienberg

This recipe is delightful for Halloween/autumn parties. They are so cute and best of all...yummy! They look like miniature taffy apples.

1/2 lb. plus 2 T. butter	1 1/2 bags (14 oz.) caramels
8 T. powdered sugar	scant 1/2 c. milk
2 egg yolks	dry roasted, finely chopped
3 c. flour	peanuts

Mix all ingredients, except caramels and milk, together and roll into small (walnut-sized) balls. Place on ungreased cookie sheet about 1" apart. Bake at 375 degrees for 12 to 15 minutes. Insert toothpicks in center. Let cool. Melt the caramels with the milk. Mix until smooth. Keep caramel on low heat. Use a wooden spoon to spoon caramel on each cookie so that it is coated completely. Roll in dry roasted, finely chopped peanuts. Put in small cookie paper cups. Makes about 75 cookies.

Lemon Chess Bars

Arlynn Geers

Bottom Layer:

1 stick butter or margarine, softened	1/4 c. confectioner's sugar
	1 c. sifted all-purpose flour

Cream butter with mixer. Add flour and sugar, mix well. Place into an 8"x8" pan and pat down. Bake at 325 degrees for 20 minutes.

Top Layer:

2 eggs	3 T. lemon juice
1 c. sugar	grated rind of 1 lemon
2 T. flour	

Beat all ingredients together. Pour over baked bottom layer (not necessary to cool bottom layer). Bake 25 minutes more or until center is set. Cool. Sprinkle with confectioner's sugar. Cut into bars. These freeze well.

Randy's Original Prize-Winning Cookies

Janet Sandall

When Randy was 7-years old, we pieced this recipe together from several others and submitted it to the Youth Fair held in Chehalis, WA. He won a first prize! Everyone loves them...even though the judges called it a "funny combination", molasses and chocolate pieces, we'd never leave them out.

1 stick (1/2 c.) margarine	1 c. flour
1 c. white sugar	1 t. cinnamon
1 egg	3/4 t. baking soda
1 T. molasses	1/4 t. salt (optional)
1 t. vanilla	1 c. quick oats

Cream together margarine and sugar. Add egg, molasses and vanilla. Combine flour, cinnamon, soda and salt; gradually add to creamed mixture. Stir in oats and add any of the optional ingredients listed below. Drop by teaspoonsful onto ungreased cookie sheet. Bake at 350 degrees for 10 to 12 minutes, or until lightly brown. Makes 3 dozen.

Optional Ingredients:

1/3 c. raisins	1/4 c. chocolate pieces
1/2 c. chopped nuts	1/2 c. coconut

Some common cookie baking problems and their solutions:

Uneven Browning - Use a shiny cookie sheet and make sure to allow at least 2" on all sides of cookie sheets in oven.

Icing Cracking - Add a pinch of baking soda to keep icing moist.

Soggy Cookies - Cool cookies on racks instead of on the pans.

Cookies Spreading - Chill dough before baking, maybe add a little more flour, and be sure to bake at the right temperature.

DiAnn Voegele

Chocolate Chocolate Chip Cookies

Gwen Blackshire

These are so very easy to make that I feel guilty when everyone raves about them! For a change, I add nuts, cherries, peanut butter pieces, raisins or sometimes I frost them.

1 devil's food cake mix
1/2 c. oil
2 eggs

1 c. chocolate chips
(or more)

Mix all ingredients. Bake on ungreased cookie sheet at 350 degrees for 10 minutes. Makes 3 1/2 dozen.

Pearls 'N Chocolate Cookies

Lois Eisenhut

2 1/4 c. flour
1 t. baking soda
1 c. (2 sticks) butter
2/3 c. firmly packed
    brown sugar
2 eggs

2/3 c. cocoa
1/2 t. salt
3/4 c. sugar
1 t. vanilla
10 oz. pkg. (1 1/2 c.) large
    white chocolate drops

Preheat oven to 350 degrees. In a small bowl combine flour, cocoa, baking soda and salt; set aside. In a large bowl, beat butter, sugar, brown sugar and vanilla until creamy. Add eggs, one at a time. Gradually add flour mixture. Stir in chocolate drops. Drop by rounded tablespoonsful onto ungreased cookie sheets. Bake for 9 to 10 minutes. Allow to stand for 2 minutes before removing from cookie sheets. Cool completely. Makes about 2 1/2 dozen large (3") cookies.

When I pack cookies to mail to my daughter, I use plain air-popped popcorn as filler in the box. It keeps cookies moist and the kids even eat the popcorn when the cookies are gone.

Cathy Weaver

Oatmeal Lover's Chocolate Chip Cookies

June Cauldwell

This weekend we just had our annual Holiday Fair at my church. I was in charge of the Bake Shop and this year I added "Cookies By the Pound". It was a huge success! Our room sold nearly $1,000.00 worth of cookies and baked goods (mostly cookies). We sold out each day (2-day fair) and had to bake on the evening of the first day late into the night to have any cookies to sell for the next day. All of my elves came through and every last cookie sold...a sellout! We were all very happy about that.

2 c. butter	5 c. old-fashioned oatmeal
2 c. brown sugar	1 t. salt
2 c. white sugar	2 t. baking soda
4 eggs	2 t. baking powder
2 t. vanilla	24 oz. pkg. chocolate chips
4 c. unbleached flour	3 c. chopped pecans

Measure out the 5 cups of oatmeal in food processor and powderize. In a bowl cream butter and sugars. Add eggs and vanilla. In a separate bowl mix flour, oatmeal, salt, baking soda and baking powder. Now mix all ingredients together, except chips and pecans; mix well. Add chocolate chips and pecans. Make golf ball-sized balls. Place 2" apart on greased cookie sheet. Flatten tops with a flat bottom glass. Bake at 350 degrees for 8 to 10 minutes. Do not overbake.

★ ☆ ★

Keep a plastic bag in the vegetable shortening can and use like a mitten when greasing pans and cookie sheets.

Ernestine Hayes

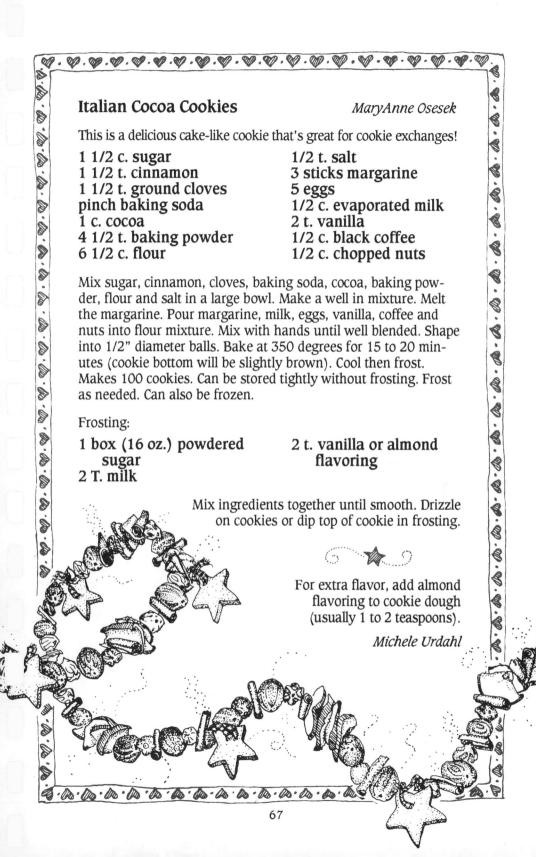

Italian Cocoa Cookies

MaryAnne Osesek

This is a delicious cake-like cookie that's great for cookie exchanges!

1 1/2 c. sugar	1/2 t. salt
1 1/2 t. cinnamon	3 sticks margarine
1 1/2 t. ground cloves	5 eggs
pinch baking soda	1/2 c. evaporated milk
1 c. cocoa	2 t. vanilla
4 1/2 t. baking powder	1/2 c. black coffee
6 1/2 c. flour	1/2 c. chopped nuts

Mix sugar, cinnamon, cloves, baking soda, cocoa, baking powder, flour and salt in a large bowl. Make a well in mixture. Melt the margarine. Pour margarine, milk, eggs, vanilla, coffee and nuts into flour mixture. Mix with hands until well blended. Shape into 1/2" diameter balls. Bake at 350 degrees for 15 to 20 minutes (cookie bottom will be slightly brown). Cool then frost. Makes 100 cookies. Can be stored tightly without frosting. Frost as needed. Can also be frozen.

Frosting:

1 box (16 oz.) powdered sugar	2 t. vanilla or almond flavoring
2 T. milk	

Mix ingredients together until smooth. Drizzle on cookies or dip top of cookie in frosting.

For extra flavor, add almond flavoring to cookie dough (usually 1 to 2 teaspoons).

Michele Urdahl

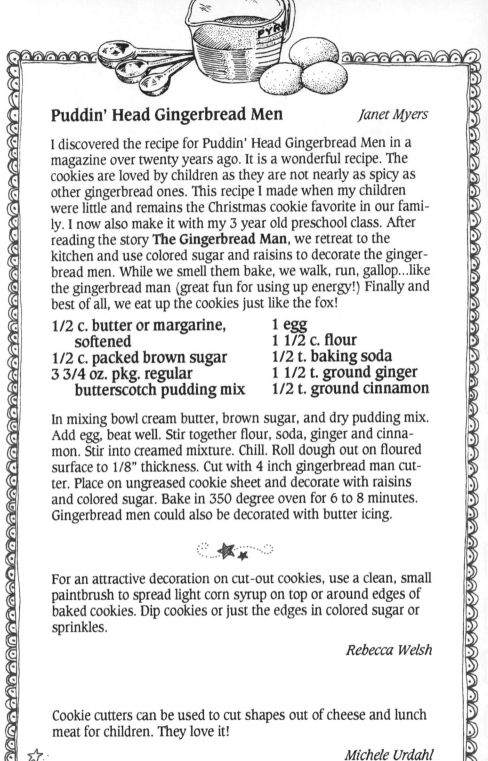

Puddin' Head Gingerbread Men   *Janet Myers*

I discovered the recipe for Puddin' Head Gingerbread Men in a
magazine over twenty years ago. It is a wonderful recipe. The
cookies are loved by children as they are not nearly as spicy as
other gingerbread ones. This recipe I made when my children
were little and remains the Christmas cookie favorite in our family. I now also make it with my 3 year old preschool class. After
reading the story **The Gingerbread Man**, we retreat to the
kitchen and use colored sugar and raisins to decorate the gingerbread men. While we smell them bake, we walk, run, gallop...like
the gingerbread man (great fun for using up energy!) Finally and
best of all, we eat up the cookies just like the fox!

1/2 c. butter or margarine, softened	1 egg
1/2 c. packed brown sugar	1 1/2 c. flour
3 3/4 oz. pkg. regular butterscotch pudding mix	1/2 t. baking soda
	1 1/2 t. ground ginger
	1/2 t. ground cinnamon

In mixing bowl cream butter, brown sugar, and dry pudding mix.
Add egg, beat well. Stir together flour, soda, ginger and cinnamon. Stir into creamed mixture. Chill. Roll dough out on floured
surface to 1/8" thickness. Cut with 4 inch gingerbread man cutter. Place on ungreased cookie sheet and decorate with raisins
and colored sugar. Bake in 350 degree oven for 6 to 8 minutes.
Gingerbread men could also be decorated with butter icing.

For an attractive decoration on cut-out cookies, use a clean, small
paintbrush to spread light corn syrup on top or around edges of
baked cookies. Dip cookies or just the edges in colored sugar or
sprinkles.

Rebecca Welsh

Cookie cutters can be used to cut shapes out of cheese and lunch
meat for children. They love it!

Michele Urdahl

Toffee Nut Bars

Mary Dungan

1/2 c. butter	1 c. flour
1/2 c. brown sugar	

Cream butter, sugar and flour together. Cover the bottom of a 9" square pan with the mixture. Bake for 10 minutes at 350 degrees. Cool.

Topping:

2 eggs	1/2 t. salt
1 c. brown sugar	1 t. vanilla
2 T. flour	1 c. coconut
1 t. baking powder	1 c. nuts

Beat together eggs and sugar, mixing well. Stir in flour, baking powder, salt, vanilla, coconut and nuts, mixing well. Spread evenly over slightly cooled first layer. Return to 350 degree oven for 35 minutes. Cool and cut.

Oatmeal Lizzies

Nancy Bogart

1 c. granulated sugar	3/4 c. brickle chips
1 c. brown sugar	1 t. baking soda
1 c. butter flavored	2 c. quick oats
shortening	1/2 c. chopped pecans
2 eggs, beaten	1/2 c. semi-sweet
1 t. vanilla	chocolate chips
2 c. flour	

Combine sugars and shortening. Add eggs and vanilla, mix well. Add flour and soda gradually, mixing well. Stir in oats, chips and pecans until will blended. Shape dough into 1 1/4" balls. Place 2" apart on greased baking sheet. Bake at 350 degrees for 12 minutes. Makes 4 1/2 dozen.

Healthful Chocolate Chip Cookies · *Jan Jacobson*

1 1/2 sticks butter,
    softened
3/4 c. brown sugar
3/4 c. white sugar
1/4 c. milk
2 eggs
1 T. vanilla
1 1/4 c. all-purpose flour

1 c. whole wheat flour
1 t. baking soda
1 t. salt
1 1/4 c. old-fashioned
    rolled oats
2 to 2 1/2 c. semi-sweet
    chocolate chips

Beat butter and sugars on high speed until fluffy. Add milk, eggs and vanilla; mix until fluffy again. Stir together all the dry ingredients, then add to butter/sugar mixture; mix well. Stir in chocolate chips with mixer on low speed. Refrigerate dough for 1 hour. Measure 2 tablespoons of dough. Roll into ball, flatten slightly and place on cookie sheet; or spoon out 2 tablespoons of dough directly on cookie sheet (just make sure dough is flattened to about 1" high). Bake in 350 degree oven until lightly browned. Cookies continue to bake on cookie sheets about 2 minutes even after you remove them from the oven. Don't overbake, or cookies will be dry. Makes about 2 dozen.

No Sugar Cookie · *Ruth Fangman*

2 c. all-purpose flour
1/2 c. butter or
    margarine
1/2 c. orange juice
1 t. grated orange peel
1/2 t. cinnamon

1/2 c. seedless raisins
1/2 c. walnuts, chopped
2 t. baking powder
1 egg
1/2 t. salt

Preheat oven to 375 degrees. In a large bowl, with wooden spoon, stir all ingredients until well mixed. Drop dough by tablespoonsful on greased cookie sheet about 2" apart. Bake 20 minutes until lightly brown. Remove from cookie sheet. Store in tightly covered container. Makes about 2 1/2 dozen. 80 calories per cookie.

Sylvia's Sour Cream Cookies

Paula Griffen

My mother made these cookies with us for the holidays and many times for no special reason, just because they are so good. I have such warm memories of making them with mom and in turn I have made them with all four of my children, passing down the warmth and love I felt growing up.

1 1/2 c. sugar
1 c. shortening
2 eggs, beaten well
1 t. soda
1 t. baking powder
1 c. sour cream
1/2 t. salt
1 t. vanilla
3 to 4 c. flour
   (enough flour to roll thin)
a little mace or nutmeg,
   if desired

Mix soda in sour cream; set aside. Mix baking powder in flour; set aside. Combine all ingredients. Chill dough a few hours or overnight. Roll out and use your favorite cookie cutters. You can leave them plain or sprinkle sugar on them, or frost them. They taste better with age. Bake at 350 degrees for 10-15 minutes.

At garage sales all year long I buy colorful tins for cookie gifts at Christmas. Using cellophane to wrap treats in, they make a perfect gift for special friends and my church family. The cost is very small compared to the new ones and are in abundance after the holidays.

Neta Liebscher

71

Ethel's Sugar Cookies

Megan Matson

When I was five I was helping my mom cook. We were making cookies. I took the beater out of the bowl and dough went everywhere. I had to help my mom clean up everything. We had to wash the pans and do everything all over again. It was not fun. But now I am 12 and I love to cook with my mom. My mom lets me cook all the time.

3/4 c. shortening	2 1/2 c. flour
1 c. sugar	1 t. baking powder
2 eggs	1 t. salt
1 t. vanilla	

Preheat oven to 400 degrees. Mix shortening, sugar and eggs. Then add all the other ingredients; mixing well. Chill for 1 hour or overnight. Roll out on floured board and cut with cookie cutters. Bake cookies 6 to 8 minutes. Decorate however you like. Makes about 2 1/2 dozen. You should make a double batch my grandmother says.

★ ☆ ☆ ☆ ★

I enjoy baking cookies and collecting cookie cutters. My collection is so varied and extensive, that I can usually dig up a suitable shaped cutter for any occasion. I especially enjoy making cookies that are whimsical or express humor. When our neighbor's children came down with chicken pox, my son and daughter thought that their best friends might need some cheering up. Together we baked cookies in the shape of chickens, and then iced them with small red dots. There were plenty of smiles when we delivered a plate of our "chicken pox cookies". When chicken pox finally caught up with our family, the same neighbors presented us with a giant gingerbread boy...clothed in icing and with those conspicuous red dots all over his face!

Kathy Nelson

Puffy Sugar Cut-Outs

Marybeth Evanko

Here is a great sugar cookie recipe. When I was a student at Penn State University, I made these in the shape of ghosts for a Halloween party. I frosted them with white icing and put on raisins for eyes. I left them on my kitchen counter overnight so the icing could dry. The next morning when I walked into the kitchen, something just didn't seem right. All the raisin eyes were gone! Upon closer inspection, there were tiny paw prints in the icing. Mice! The cookies were too fat to fit in the mouse hole, so they just took the raisins. Too bad, because these cookies are delicious!

3 1/4 c. flour	1 c. sugar
1 t. baking soda	1 egg
1/2 t. salt	1 1/2 t. vanilla
1/2 t. nutmeg	1/2 c. sour cream
1/2 c. butter, softened	

Combine dry ingredients; set aside. Cream butter. Add sugar, egg and vanilla; beat well. Beat in sour cream. Gradually add dry ingredients. If dough is not stiff enough to roll out, wrap in plastic wrap and chill for 1 hour. Roll out on a lightly floured surface to 1/4" thickness. Cut with cookie cutter. Bake on lightly greased cookie sheets at 400 degrees for 8 to 10 minutes. Yield depends on size of cutter used. Decorate as desired.

✰★☆★☆

I never bother to roll out cookies (or pie crust) on a wooden board or a cloth. I just sprinkle my formica countertop with flour and away I go. Easy clean-up too!

Tamara Gruber

Lebkuchen (Honey Cookies)

Elaine Harris Myers

My grandmother came here as a young girl from Germany. By the time I was old enough to really know her well, she was in her seventies. We would make these cookies together and I could tell even then that it made her a little homesick. She would tell me stories of her German childhood while I did all the stirring. She wasn't strong enough any more to do the mixing, so that was my job. It has been almost 20 years ago since we made cookies together, but they will always remind me of her and how kind she was to me. The recipe makes a large amount, and she would store them in coffee cans and they would last my grandparents for many months.

1 qt. strained honey
6 1/4 c. flour
6 eggs
2 1/2 c. sugar
2 T. cinnamon
1 T. cloves

1 T. allspice
1 T. nutmeg
2 T. lemon juice
1 T. baking soda
4 3/4 c. flour

Warm the honey until thin and runny. Stir in the 6 1/4 cups of flour and set aside. Beat eggs until light and thick. Add sugar and beat well by hand. Stir in spices. Mix lemon juice and soda and stir into mixture. Add 4 3/4 cup flour. Then mix in honey and flour mixture. (Mixture is very, very thick.) Let stand in bowl, covered overnight. Drop by tablespoonsful on lightly greased cookie sheet. Bake at 350 degrees for 8 to 10 minutes. When cool, ice with powdered sugar and beaten egg white icing and press one almond in center of each cookie. Store in tightly covered container.

Each Christmas, one of the gifts I give my children and husband is a tin of their favorite home baked cookies. They always look forward to this special gift.

Marcia Latimer

London Fog Bars

Mrs. Donald Herbert

First Layer:

1/2 c. butter
1/2 c. sugar
1 egg
5 T. cocoa
1 t. vanilla

2 c. crushed graham
   cracker (about 22)
1 c. flaked coconut
1/2 c. chopped nuts

Combine in top of a double boiler the butter, sugar, egg, cocoa and vanilla. Cook over hot water for 10 minutes or until a soft ball forms in cold water. Avoid cooking too long or getting too hot as the butter will separate. Stir in the cracker crumbs, coconut and nuts. Pour into an ungreased 9"x9" pan.

Second Layer:

1/4 c. butter
3 T. cream

3 T. vanilla instant pudding
2 c. powdered sugar

Mix all ingredients together and spread over the first layer.

Third Layer:

1 oz. square German chocolate
3- 1 oz. squares semi-sweet
   chocolate
1 T. butter

Melt and spread over cooled layers. Store in cool place.

When I moved to Florida, I was home-sick; my husband's boss invited me to her house to help her bake Christmas cookies. It was so enjoyable. It's fun to experience different baking styles and learn new recipes.

Koni Updyke

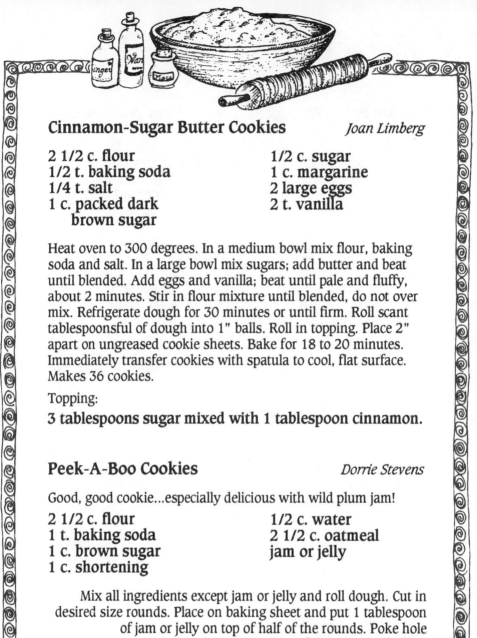

Cinnamon-Sugar Butter Cookies

Joan Limberg

2 1/2 c. flour
1/2 t. baking soda
1/4 t. salt
1 c. packed dark
　brown sugar

1/2 c. sugar
1 c. margarine
2 large eggs
2 t. vanilla

Heat oven to 300 degrees. In a medium bowl mix flour, baking soda and salt. In a large bowl mix sugars; add butter and beat until blended. Add eggs and vanilla; beat until pale and fluffy, about 2 minutes. Stir in flour mixture until blended, do not over mix. Refrigerate dough for 30 minutes or until firm. Roll scant tablespoonsful of dough into 1" balls. Roll in topping. Place 2" apart on ungreased cookie sheets. Bake for 18 to 20 minutes. Immediately transfer cookies with spatula to cool, flat surface. Makes 36 cookies.

Topping:

3 tablespoons sugar mixed with 1 tablespoon cinnamon.

Peek-A-Boo Cookies

Dorrie Stevens

Good, good cookie...especially delicious with wild plum jam!

2 1/2 c. flour
1 t. baking soda
1 c. brown sugar
1 c. shortening

1/2 c. water
2 1/2 c. oatmeal
jam or jelly

Mix all ingredients except jam or jelly and roll dough. Cut in desired size rounds. Place on baking sheet and put 1 tablespoon of jam or jelly on top of half of the rounds. Poke hole with thumb in the centers of the other half of the rounds. Place a round with a hole on top of each round topped with jam or jelly. Press edges with a fork. Bake at 350 degrees for 12 minutes.

Cream Wafers

Marion Pfeifer

1 c. butter, softened
1/3 c. cream (35% butter fat)
2 c. sifted flour

Mix well butter, cream and flour; chill. Heat oven to 375 degrees. Roll out dough to 1/8" thick on floured board. Cut with 1 1/2" cutter. Roll only 1/3 of dough at a time, keeping the rest of the dough refrigerated. Transfer rounds to waxed paper heavily covered with granulated sugar. Turn each round so that both sides are coated with sugar. Place on ungreased cookie sheet. Prick with fork about four times. Bake 7 to 9 minutes. Cool and put two cookies together with filling. Makes about 5 dozen double cookies.

Filling:

1/4 c. butter, softened
3/4 c. sifted confectioner's
   sugar

1 egg yolk
1 t. vanilla

Blend all ingredients together, then tint pink or green.

Use your cookie cutters for cutting out tea sandwiches. Mix cream cheese with fresh herbs, spread between two pieces of cocktail bread and cut out hearts, bells, stars ...whatever suits the occasion!

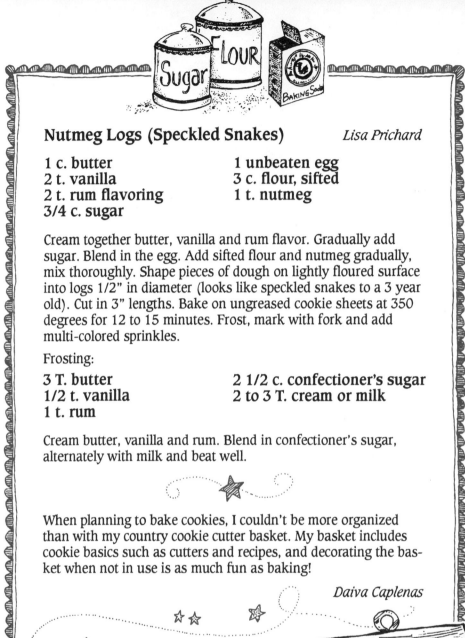

Nutmeg Logs (Speckled Snakes)   *Lisa Prichard*

1 c. butter	1 unbeaten egg
2 t. vanilla	3 c. flour, sifted
2 t. rum flavoring	1 t. nutmeg
3/4 c. sugar	

Cream together butter, vanilla and rum flavor. Gradually add sugar. Blend in the egg. Add sifted flour and nutmeg gradually, mix thoroughly. Shape pieces of dough on lightly floured surface into logs 1/2" in diameter (looks like speckled snakes to a 3 year old). Cut in 3" lengths. Bake on ungreased cookie sheets at 350 degrees for 12 to 15 minutes. Frost, mark with fork and add multi-colored sprinkles.

Frosting:

3 T. butter	2 1/2 c. confectioner's sugar
1/2 t. vanilla	2 to 3 T. cream or milk
1 t. rum	

Cream butter, vanilla and rum. Blend in confectioner's sugar, alternately with milk and beat well.

When planning to bake cookies, I couldn't be more organized than with my country cookie cutter basket. My basket includes cookie basics such as cutters and recipes, and decorating the basket when not in use is as much fun as baking!

Daiva Caplenas

Cookie Cutters

Peanut Butter Temptations

Lisa Prichard

1/2 c. butter or margarine, softened
1/2 c. creamy peanut butter
1/2 c. sugar
1/2 c. brown sugar
1 egg
1/2 t. vanilla
1/2 t. salt
1 1/4 c. flour
3/4 t. baking soda
48 mini peanut butter filled chocolate candies

Cream butter and peanut butter. Gradually add sugar, beat until light and fluffy. Add egg and vanilla. Combine dry ingredients. Add to creamed mixture. Chill dough for 1 hour. Shape dough into 48 1" balls. Place in lightly greased 1 3/4" muffin pans, shaping each into a shell. Bake at 350 degrees for 12 minutes (dough will rise during baking). Remove from oven and immediately press peanut butter candy evenly into each hot crust. Cool before removing from pan (very important).

Danish Spice Cookies

Jennifer Muller

2 c. sifted all-purpose flour
1/2 t. salt
1/4 t. baking soda
1 t. ground cinnamon
1/4 t. ground clove
1/2 c. butter or margarine
1 c. firmly packed brown sugar
1/2 c. dairy sour cream
1 egg
1 t. vanilla
1/2 c. chopped walnuts
1 c. chopped dates

Preheat oven to 350 degrees. Sift flour, salt, baking soda, cinnamon and cloves onto waxed paper. Melt butter in a medium-sized saucepan over moderate heat. Add sugar and beat with a wooden spoon until combined. Beat in sour cream, egg and vanilla until smooth. Stir in flour mixture until thoroughly combined. Stir in dates and nuts. Spread evenly into a greased 15"x10"x1" pan. Bake for 30 minutes or until top springs up. Makes 4 dozen.

Cookie making and I have had a long and wonderful relationship. Making cookies with my aunt and grandmother dances through my childhood memories and has often been the focus of free time activity in my adult life. I was born in Germany during World War II and came to America as a five year old with an ongoing, serious respiratory illness that was to be healed with antibiotics, rest and time. My grandmother opened her home to our family and she and my aunt gave hours of their time keeping me amused and quiet. Cookie making became a love...I adored making cookies! Each afternoon before my nap, I participated (minimally) in the making of the dough and was allowed to pat it before I went off for a nap, being assured that when I awoke from a "good rest" that I could roll out, cut out, decorate and bake these cookies. If my aunt was involved, we made sugar cookies. My grandmother loved molasses or ginger cookies and she and I made those, decorating them with cinnamon red hots. She called them "Monkey Faces." As I look back (with adult eyes) to the sticky kitchen, dough globs on the floor, and decorations everywhere...the mess which I created every afternoon for over one year, I remember being in heaven because I was making cookies. Today I feel blessed knowing how much these two women loved me and cared for me. The scent of ginger and cinnamon always brings me back to my grandmother's kitchen and those wonderful cookies. I now have my grandmother's and great grandmother's handwritten cookbooks. I found a little bit of history in one of them...in the late 1800's, women always baked and had on hand two kinds of cookies...cookies made with brown sugar and/or molasses, for the family, and those made with white sugar and white flour, generally rolled out, for company only.

Christel Fishburn

80

Patrick's Chocolate Brownies

Anne Farnese

Baking cookies is a favorite past-time I've enjoyed for more than thirty years. Although I make a wide variety of cookies, chocolate brownies are the best loved and most requested. During the month of December, I fill small holiday treat bags with these delicious brownies. I arrange the bags on a tray and keep it near the front door to have on hand as a holiday surprise for service and delivery people. Last year I gave a bag of brownies to our twelve year old paperboy, Patrick, when he collected our monthly payment. Two days later he returned, and nervously inquired as to whether or not I had paid him because our name wasn't checked off in his record book. "Don't you remember? I gave you a bag of brownies when I paid you," I said, pointing to the tray. His freckle-covered face reddened and he sheepishly admitted he hadn't told the truth. "I just had to have another bag of those awesome brownies!" he blurted out. His roundabout compliment warmed my heart and I handed him an extra bag as a reward for his honesty, along with the admonishment to "just ask next time." I hope you enjoy the brownies as much as Patrick!

3/4 c. cocoa	1 t. pure vanilla extract
3/4 c. shortening	1 1/4 c. flour
2 1/4 c. sugar	1 t. baking powder
4 large eggs	1 t. salt

Heat the oven to 350 degrees and grease a 13"x9"x2" baking pan. Melt shortening in a large saucepan over low heat, then stir in cocoa. Remove from heat. Mix in sugar and vanilla, then mix in eggs one at at time. Stir in remaining ingredients. Bake for 30 minutes. Cool completely before cutting into 2"x2" squares. Makes approximately 28 brownies.

Cut out heart in hand cookies and dip the finger tips in chocolate.

Sally Clarno

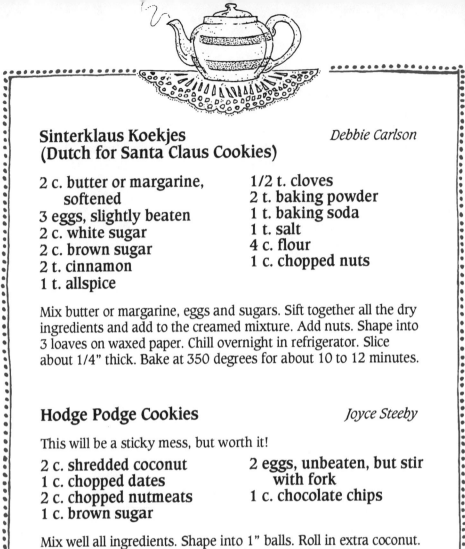

Sinterklaus Koekjes
(Dutch for Santa Claus Cookies)

Debbie Carlson

2 c. butter or margarine,
  softened
3 eggs, slightly beaten
2 c. white sugar
2 c. brown sugar
2 t. cinnamon
1 t. allspice

1/2 t. cloves
2 t. baking powder
1 t. baking soda
1 t. salt
4 c. flour
1 c. chopped nuts

Mix butter or margarine, eggs and sugars. Sift together all the dry ingredients and add to the creamed mixture. Add nuts. Shape into 3 loaves on waxed paper. Chill overnight in refrigerator. Slice about 1/4" thick. Bake at 350 degrees for about 10 to 12 minutes.

Hodge Podge Cookies

Joyce Steeby

This will be a sticky mess, but worth it!

2 c. shredded coconut
1 c. chopped dates
2 c. chopped nutmeats
1 c. brown sugar

2 eggs, unbeaten, but stir
  with fork
1 c. chocolate chips

Mix well all ingredients. Shape into 1" balls. Roll in extra coconut. Bake at 350 degrees for 10 to 12 minutes. Cool completely on cookie sheet before removing. Keep in airtight container.

When baking cookies for a child's party, I put an edible surprise (miniature marshmallow, candied cherry, pinch of sprinkles, cluster of mint, butterscotch or chocolate chips) in the center of one spoonful of dough. Whoever eats the cookie with the surprise wins a small toy.

Elizabeth Ray

Grandma Sour's Stuffed Date Drops

Sheila Kennedy

When I married my husband, I was lucky to gain a wonderful grandma. This cookie recipe is one of our favorites...from grandma. Her health no longer permits her to do a lot of baking like she used to do every day when she lived on her farm.

1 lb. pitted dates	1 1/4 c. flour
3 oz. pkg. pecans	1/2 t. baking powder
1/4 c. shortening	1/2 t. baking soda
3/4 c. brown sugar	1/4 t. salt
1 egg	1/2 c. sour cream

Stuff dates with pecan meats. Cream shortening and sugar until light; beat in egg. Add dry ingredients alternately with sour cream to the creamed mixture. Stir in dates, drop onto greased cookie sheet (one date per cookie). Bake in hot oven (350 degrees) for 8 to 12 minutes. Let cool.

Golden Frosting:

1/2 c. butter	3/4 t. vanilla
3 c. powdered sugar	

Lightly brown butter, remove from heat. Beat in powdered sugar and vanilla. Slowly add warm water until of spreading consistency.

★

When freezing cookies with a frosting, place them in the freezer, unwrapped, for about 2 hours. Then wrap without worrying that they will stick together.

DiAnn Voegele

Baker's Christmas Cookies

Shirley Baker

4 oz. cream cheese,
   softened
1/2 c. butter, softened
1 c. flour

1/2 lb. pecan halves
1 bag caramels
12 oz. bag chocolate chips
non-pareils

Place softened cream cheese and butter in a bowl. Gradually add flour to form a dough. Chill dough in the refrigerator. Roll out and cut with 2" circle cutter. Place on ungreased cookie sheet and bake at 400 degrees for 12 minutes. Remove from oven, place 1/2 pecan onto each circle of pastry. Place an unwrapped caramel on top of each pecan. Return cookies to oven and watch closely. Remove from oven when caramels have melted. Lightly flatten caramels with a buttered knife. Melt chocolate chips in a double boiler or microwave. Stir chips and spread on top of each melted caramel. Sprinkle non-pareils on top of warm melted chocolate.

Kaneel Koekjes (Cinnamon Snaps)

Jennifer Muller

1 c. sugar
1 c. shortening
1 c. molasses
2 t. baking soda, dissolved
   in 2 T. warm water
6 c. cake flour
1 T. cinnamon
1 T. ginger
1/2 t. salt

Preheat oven to 350 degrees. Cream sugar with shortening; add molasses, then baking soda dissolved in water. Sift together flour, cinnamon, ginger and salt; add to creamed mixture. These cookies can either be rolled out very thin or can be patted out on a cookie sheet and baked 8 to 10 minutes. Makes 6 dozen cookies.

Caramel Brownie Tarts

Lisa Prichard

1/2 c. butter or margarine,
  softened
1 c. sugar
2 large eggs
2 oz. unsweetened
  chocolate, melted

1 t. vanilla extract
1/2 t. salt
1 c. flour, sifted
36 chocolate covered
  caramels

Heat oven to 350 degrees. Place mini foil or paper backing cups in miniature cupcake tins (36 total). Beat butter until creamy. On low speed, beat in sugar, eggs, melted chocolate, vanilla and salt. Gradually beat in flour. Divide batter into baking cups using 1 level tablespoon per cup. Bake 10 to 12 minutes until almost done. Press one candy, bottom side up, into the center of each tart until even with top. Cool in pans on wire racks 10 minutes. Remove from tins and cool. Makes 36.

Christmas Cookie Centerpiece

A fun way to use your cookie cutters is to make a Christmas cookie centerpiece. Make a batch of gingerbread, and a batch of sugar cookies, increasing the amount of flour by 1/2 cup in each recipe since the cookies are going to be handled a good deal and a firmer dough is preferable. Even with the extra flour, the cookies are still good to eat. Cut a variety of shapes such as bells, stars, stockings, trees and santas. Before baking, make a small hole at the top of each cookie. When cookies are cool, use a decorating bag filled with icing to fill in the features or outline the shapes made by the cutters. With beaded dressmaker's pins, attach cookies to a styrofoam cone (I use a 12" tall 7" diameter cone). Start pinning with the bottom row of cookies, then move to the row above. Arrange the cookies so they overlap slightly. End with a star at the top. To make the tree more festive, fill in the spaces with little red bows and holly leaves.

Marsha Jones

Cookie Pizza

Michelle Riley

1/2 c. powdered sugar
1/2 c. sugar
1/2 c. vegetable oil
1/2 c. margarine, softened
1 egg

1/2 t. vanilla
2 c. plus 2 T. flour
1/2 t. soda
1/2 t. salt

Toppings:

coconut, chocolate chips, marshmallows, cinnamon or brown sugar.

Mix sugars, oil and margarine in a large bowl. Stir in egg and vanilla. Combine flour, soda and salt; gradually blend into mixture. Using hands, press dough onto round pizza pan. Bake at 375 degrees until almost done, but not browned; remove from oven. Spread toppings of your choice over cookie, return to oven and bake until cookie is slightly browned. Let cool, cut like a pizza.

Cookie Welcome

Like the strips of suckers at the store, one day I decided why not package cookies like that? Begin by laying a long strip of plastic wrap on the table. Lay decorated gingerbread boy cookies face down, pull the wrap from both sides over the cookies. Tie a bow between each cookie and hang the strip by your door. I've done this for years and our boys and girls love it. As they go out the door, a cookie is snipped off and goes with them. It looks great and adds a Christmasy welcome to our home.

Pat Eveland

Save leftover icing from cakes, etc., and freeze in plastic wrap. You can then use your accumulated dabs of icing to frost cookies by allowing frostings to warm to room temperature. A sweet recycling tidbit!

Judy Hand

Pepparkakor
(Swedish Ginger Cookies)

Karin Swanson

1 1/2 c. sifted flour
1 1/2 t. ginger
1/4 t. ground cloves
1 t. baking soda
1 t. cinnamon

1/2 c. butter or margarine
3/4 c. sugar
1 egg, beaten well
1 1/2 t. dark corn syrup

Sift together the flour, ginger, cloves, baking soda and cinnamon; set aside. Cream butter until softened; add sugar gradually, beating thoroughly. Combine egg and corn syrup. Blend egg mixture into sugar and butter. Blend in dry ingredients in fourths, mixing thoroughly after each addition. Chill for several hours. Remove small amount of chilled dough and place on lightly floured surface. Roll to 1/16" thick (very thin). Cut with lightly floured cookie cutters. Bake at 375 degrees for 6 to 7 minutes.

Tips: Roll as thin as possible, the thinner the better. Also, when rolling out, use as little flour on surface as you can so cookies stay light and crisp. Don't overcook. Okay to freeze.

Legend has it that if you tap on one with your knuckle and if it breaks in 3 pieces, you'll have good luck for the coming year!

87

Mandel Skorpor
(Swedish Biscuit Cookie)

Karin Swanson

Great for coffee or tea dunking!

1 c. sugar
1/2 c. butter
1 egg
1/2 c. cream or milk

2 heaping t. baking
  powder
3 1/2 c. flour
4 t. almond extract

Blend sugar, butter, egg and cream or milk. Add baking powder, flour and almond extract. Make 2 rolls (logs). Bake at 350 degrees for 25 to 30 minutes. After baking, cut diagonally and slow dry in oven, with the door open, at 200 degrees for approximately 2 hours.

Zucchini-Lemon Cookies

Valerie Thompson

2 c. flour
1 t. baking powder
1/2 t. salt
3/4 c. butter or margarine
3/4 c. sugar

1 egg, beaten
1 t. (or more) lemon peel
1 c. shredded unpeeled
  zucchini
1 c. chopped nuts

Sift together dry ingredients and set aside. Cream butter and sugar. Add egg and lemon peel. Add dry ingredients; stir until smooth. Add nuts and zucchini. Drop by teaspoonful onto greased sheet. Bake at 375 degrees for 15 minutes. Remove from baking sheets to cool. If desired, sift confectioner's sugar over tops. Makes 4 dozen.

★ ☆ ★

Ever since we first saw a Scandinavian cookie tree, one of our favorite decorations is making cut-out cookies to hang on this tree. Every year, we change the shape. One year was gingerbread boys, then it was gnomes, then angels. Visitors get to pick a cookie when they leave. We also use our cookie tree for valentines, spring and autumn cookie shapes.

Elenna Firme
Gooseberry Patch Artisan

Pecan Log Roll

Mary Jo Baird

7 oz. jar marshmallow
   cream
1 lb. powdered sugar
1 t. vanilla

14 oz. pkg. caramels
3 T. water
1 1/2 c. chopped pecans

Combine marshmallow cream, sugar and vanilla. Shape into 4"x1" rolls. Chill for 2 to 3 hours. Combine caramels and water in double boiler and melt. Dip rolls into melted caramel and roll in pecans. Chill for 1 hour, then cut into slices.

Cookie Mold Ornaments

I recently learned a wonderful new way to use my cookie molds and old candle stubs to make delightful ornaments. You will need:

cookie molds
candle stubs
oil (spray-on is easiest)

crayons (in desired colors)
a double boiler or two pans

Oil the molds and freeze or refrigerate for approximately 20 minutes (make sure your mold is freezer-safe before putting it in the freezer). Melt the wax by putting it in the smaller of your two pans or the bottom of your double boiler, over simmering water. Add the crayons (to brighten colored wax and to add color to white wax). Be very careful with the wax...do not overheat or you may risk fire, also avoid touching the hot wax and please keep young children away to avoid burns. Carefully pour the wax into your mold. After the wax hardens a little, put the mold in the freezer to speed the cooling process. They can then be painted with acrylic paints. Scented candles make the ornaments even more pleasant. You could even use beeswax...the honey fragrance is delicious! Make holes in the ornaments with a tool used for picking nut meats. Heat the tool in hot water and carefully press into the melted wax. An ice pick or a wire would also work.

Mary-Gail King

Buttermilk Cookies

Kay Oglageo

1/2 c. shortening
1/2 c. butter
2 eggs, beaten
1 1/2 c. sugar
1 c. buttermilk
3 c. flour plus 3 T.

1/2 t. nutmeg
1 t. soda
1 t. vanilla
1 t. baking soda
pinch of salt

Cream shortening, butter and sugar well. Add eggs and vanilla. Stir soda into buttermilk. Sift flour, baking soda, salt and nutmeg together. Add the buttermilk alternately with the dry ingredients to the creamed mixture. Drop by teaspoonsful onto a sprayed cookie sheet. Bake at 325 degrees for 15 minutes or until light brown on top.

Icing:

1 stick butter
1/2 c. shortening
1 t. vanilla

1 small bag
   confectioner's sugar
1 T. milk

Mix ingredients well. Add food coloring if you wish. If not thick enough, add more sugar.

Biscotti Cookies

Janice Ertola

2 c. plus 3 T. flour
2 t. baking powder
1/4 t. salt
1/4 c. margarine
1 c. sugar

3 eggs
1 T. almond extract or
   anise extract
1 pkg. slivered almonds

Beat margarine and sugar until light, add each egg and beat well after each. Beat in extract. Combine flour, baking powder and salt; add to sugar mixture at low speed. Divide batter in half. Spread half onto separate greased baking sheets, in the shape of a long narrow loaf of bread. Bake at 375 degrees for 15 to 20 minutes or until golden brown. Remove from pan, cut into 1" slices, turn on sides and bake an additional 10 to 15 minutes. Cool on a rack.

Cherry Macaroons

Valerie Thompson

1 c. shortening
1 c. sugar
3 eggs
1/2 c. dairy sour cream
3 c. flour
1 t. baking powder

1/2 t. soda
1/2 t. salt
2/3 c. candied cherries
1 c. shredded coconut
1 t. grated lemon rind
1 1/2 t. almond extract

Mix shortening, sugar and eggs thoroughly. Stir in sour cream. Mix dry ingredients together and add to creamed mixture. Fold in cut up cherries, coconut, rind and extract. Drop on ungreased cookie sheet. Bake at 400 degrees for 10 to 12 minutes. Remove from cookie sheet to cool.

Black Bottoms

Karin Swanson

Black Mix:

1 1/2 c. flour
1/4 c. cocoa
1 t. baking soda
1 c. sugar
1/2 t. salt

1 c. water
1 t. vinegar
1/2 c. oil
1 t. vanilla

Combine flour, cocoa, sugar, salt and baking soda. Add water, vinegar, oil and vanilla; set aside.

White Mix:

1 egg
8 oz. cream cheese
1/3 c. sugar
1/8 t. salt
1 c. mini chocolate chips

Beat egg until fluffy. Add cream cheese, sugar and salt; mixing well. Stir in chocolate chips. Using mini muffin paper cups (1 3/4" diameter) fill cupcake liners 1/2 full of black mix, put about 3/4 teaspoon white mix on top. Bake at 350 degrees for 20 minutes. Bake on cookie sheets.

Chocolate Butternuts

Jennifer Bolton

1/2 c. butter
1/2 c. powdered sugar
1/4 t. salt

1 t. vanilla
1 to 1 1/4 c. flour

Cream butter and sugar; add salt and vanilla. Cream well. Add flour. Shape into balls. Place on ungreased cookie sheets. Press hole in each. Bake at 350 degrees for 10 to 15 minutes. Fill while warm. Cool. Frost. Makes 2 dozen.

Filling:

3 oz. cream cheese
1 c. powdered sugar
2 T. flour

1 t. vanilla
1/2 c. chopped walnuts
1/2 c. coconut

Blend cream cheese, sugar, flour and vanilla. Stir in walnuts and coconut.

Frosting:

1/2 c. chocolate chips
2 T. butter

2 T. water
1/2 c. powdered sugar

Melt over hot water the chocolate chips, butter and water; stirring occasionally. Add powdered sugar, beat until smooth.

Coconut Meringue Cookies

Barbara McCaffrey

My kids call these "magic cookies."

1 box regular angel
   food cake mix
1/2 c. water

1 t. vanilla
2 c. coconut

Whip egg white packet with water and vanilla until stiff. Fold in dry ingredients packet and coconut. Line cookie sheets with tin foil. Drop by teaspoonsful 2" apart on cookie sheet. Bake at 350 degrees for 12 minutes. Remove cookies from foil when completely cooled. Makes 4 to 5 dozen.

Lace Roll-Ups

Jennifer Bolton

1 c. flour
1 c. finely chopped nuts
1/2 c. corn syrup

1/2 c. shortening
2/3 c. packed brown sugar

Heat oven to 375 degrees. Mix flour and nuts. In a medium saucepan heat corn syrup, shortening and sugar to boiling, over medium heat, stirring constantly. Remove from heat; gradually stir in flour/nut mixture. Drop dough by teaspoonsful about 3" apart onto lightly greased baking sheet. Bake only 8 or 9 cookies at one time. Bake about 5 minutes; cool for 3 minutes before removing from baking sheet. While warm, carefully roll cookies into cylindrical shapes. If cookies harden before shaping, return them to the oven for just a moment. Makes about 4 dozen cookies. For chocolate dipped cookies, dip one end of the lace roll-ups in melted semi-sweet chocolate. Let cool.

To soften cookies that become a little hard, just put an apple slice on waxed paper and place it in the container of cookies. Remove after one day.

Michele Urdahl

Stencil and decorate brown paper lunchbags and fill with holiday cookies. For a fun touch, tie recipe on with red ribbon and a sprig of evergreen!

Soft Drop Jewels

Jennifer Bolton

1 c. shortening
2 c. sugar
2 eggs
1 1/2 c. buttermilk
2 t. vanilla

1/2 t. lemon extract
4 c. flour
1 t. soda
1 t. salt

Cream shortening, sugar and eggs until light and fluffy. Beat in buttermilk, vanilla and lemon extract. Sift the flour, soda and salt; stir into batter. Drop by rounded teaspoonful onto cookie sheet. Bake at 400 degrees for 8 to 10 minutes. Cookies should be brown around edges, not center. Frost. Decorate with a red candied cherry half and two green candied cherry pieces on each side.

Frosting:

1/4 lb. butter or margarine
1/4 c. milk
1/4 t. salt

1 lb. powdered sugar
1 t. vanilla

Beat at low speed until ingredients are blended, then beat on high speed for five minutes.

I remember baking Christmas cookies with my mother and my great aunt. On one occasion we had finished cleaning up and had just sat down to have a cookie. I don't recall what made my aunt tell us this, but she told me a story of a time in her life when she was young and alone. She had enough money to pay for a room in a woman's house, but not enough to buy food. She hadn't eaten in a couple of days when she asked the woman if she could work in exchange for something to eat. My aunt put in a hard day's work and was rewarded with a bowl of soup and some bread. Her eyes welled up as she told me, "That was the best food I had ever eaten." Some 50 years later that still brought her pain. Every year when I bake Christmas cookies, I think of Aunt Ethel and the story she told me. That story is a part of Christmas baking for me and a wonderful reminder of all that I have to be thankful for. The magic of Christmas cookies!

Connie Tumm

Oatmeal-Carrot Cookies

Barbara McCaffrey

A healthy, high-fiber treat even kids love!

1 c. flour
1/2 t. baking soda
1 1/2 c. uncooked oats
1 t. cinnamon
2 eggs, slightly beaten
1/2 c. brown sugar
1/3 c. oil (preferably
    safflower or canola)

1/2 c. nonfat or lowfat
    milk
1 t. vanilla
1 c. raisins
1 c. grated carrots
1 c. chopped nuts
    (optional)

Sift together flour, baking soda and cinnamon. Stir in oats. Combine eggs, brown sugar, milk, vanilla, raisins, carrots and oil; add to the flour mixture and mix well. Add nuts. Drop by teaspoonful onto lightly oiled cookie sheet. Bake at 375 degrees for 12 to 15 minutes, depending on texture desired. Shorter baking time results in a chewy, soft cookie, longer baking time results in a crisper cookie. Makes 3 dozen cookies, 70 calories per cookie.

Recipe for Christmas Cookies

Light oven, get bowl, spoons and ingredients; grease pan; crack nuts; remove 10 blocks, seven toy autos and one wad of chewing gum from kitchen table. Measure 2 cups of flour; remove Johnny's hands from flour, wash flour off him, measure 1 more cup of flour to replace flour on floor. Put flour, baking powder and salt in sifter. Answer doorbell. Return to kitchen. Remove Johnny's hands from bowl. Wash Johnny. Answer phone; return. Remove 1/4 inch salt from greased pans. Grease more pans. Look for Johnny. Answer phone. Return to kitchen and find Johnny. Remove his hands from bowl. Wash shortening, etc. off him. Take up greased pans and find nut shells in it. Head for Johnny who flees, knocking bowl off table. Wash kitchen floor. Wash table. Wash kitchen walls. Wash dishes. Wash Johnny. Call bakery.

Charlotte Worlitz

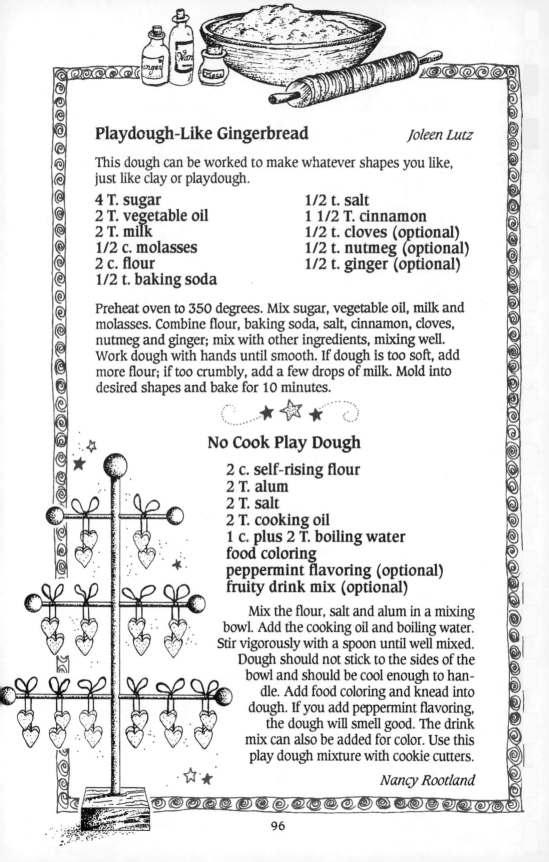

Playdough-Like Gingerbread

Joleen Lutz

This dough can be worked to make whatever shapes you like, just like clay or playdough.

4 T. sugar
2 T. vegetable oil
2 T. milk
1/2 c. molasses
2 c. flour
1/2 t. baking soda

1/2 t. salt
1 1/2 T. cinnamon
1/2 t. cloves (optional)
1/2 t. nutmeg (optional)
1/2 t. ginger (optional)

Preheat oven to 350 degrees. Mix sugar, vegetable oil, milk and molasses. Combine flour, baking soda, salt, cinnamon, cloves, nutmeg and ginger; mix with other ingredients, mixing well. Work dough with hands until smooth. If dough is too soft, add more flour; if too crumbly, add a few drops of milk. Mold into desired shapes and bake for 10 minutes.

No Cook Play Dough

2 c. self-rising flour
2 T. alum
2 T. salt
2 T. cooking oil
1 c. plus 2 T. boiling water
food coloring
peppermint flavoring (optional)
fruity drink mix (optional)

Mix the flour, salt and alum in a mixing bowl. Add the cooking oil and boiling water. Stir vigorously with a spoon until well mixed. Dough should not stick to the sides of the bowl and should be cool enough to handle. Add food coloring and knead into dough. If you add peppermint flavoring, the dough will smell good. The drink mix can also be added for color. Use this play dough mixture with cookie cutters.

Nancy Rootland

Better-Than-Tollhouse Chocolate Chip Hearts

Joleen Lutz

1 c. butter
1/2 c. granulated sugar
1 c. brown sugar, packed
2 eggs, beaten
1 T. vanilla
1/2 t. salt
3/4 t. baking powder
2 c. flour
1/2 c. quick-cooking oats

12 oz. (scant 2 c.) semi-sweet chocolate chips
6 oz. milk chocolate chips (scant 1 c.) or bar, broken
1 c. chopped roasted almonds or walnuts
melted chocolate (optional)

Cream butter until light. Beat in granulated sugar and brown sugar. Add beaten eggs, vanilla, salt and baking powder; mix well. Add flour and oats and mix well. Fold in semi-sweet and milk chocolate chips, then the nuts. Spoon dough into greased and floured small heart-shaped (disposable foil pans work well) cake pans (about 1/3 to 1/2 cup dough for 4" to 5" heart pans). Bake at 350 degrees for 12 to 15 minutes or until lightly browned. Bake longer if filling pans more fully for cake-like cookies. Or, drop dough by large spoonfuls onto greased baking sheet and bake at 350 degrees for 10 minutes. Let stand for 5 minutes in pans then cut along side with knife and turn over pan, tapping lightly on center of pan until released. Let cool. If desired, frost with melted chocolate. Makes 20 to 24 large heart cookies or 4 dozen round cookies.

I have given frozen cookie dough to friends for holiday gifts. That way, they can enjoy cookies fresh from the oven any time they want!

Teresa German

Butter Horn Cookies

Linda Ferguson

1 lb. butter or margarine
1 1/4 c. buttermilk
4 c. flour

4 t. vanilla
2 egg yolks

Mix the above ingredients. Separate into three rolls and refrigerate overnight. Cut each roll into fourths and roll out each fourth into a circle and cut like a pizza into twelve sections.

Cookie Filling:

3/4 c. brown sugar
1 c. sugar

2 t. cinnamon
1 c. walnuts

Combine ingredients and fill the triangle slice at large end and roll to the small end. Ice cookies while warm with frosting made from powdered sugar, butter, vanilla and water. Bake at 375 degrees for 10 to 12 minutes.

Unbaked Fudge Drops

Dianna Mesnard

30 individual graham
    cracker squares
2 c. white sugar
1 c. evaporated milk
2 T. butter

2 squares chocolate
24 marshmallows
    cut in squares
1/2 c. chopped pecans

Combine sugar, chocolate, evaporated milk and butter in a large saucepan. Bring to a boil very slowly and stir constantly until sugar is completely dissolved. Boil slowly for 5 minutes, stirring occasionally. Cool to lukewarm. Crush crackers very fine. Add the marshmallows, crumbs and nuts to chocolate mixture. Stir until crumbs are thoroughly blended. Drop by teaspoonful on waxed paper. Top with pecan halves. Let stand until firm, about 2 hours.

Mix sugar and cinnamon together in shaker to sprinkle on cookies before baking.

Mrs. Travis Baker

Raspberry Almond Squares

Theresa Smith

These cookies are light and buttery. I especially enjoy them during the holidays because of the different flavor the raspberry jam gives them. Best of all, they are quick and easy to make.

1 c. butter
1 c. sugar
1 egg
1/2 t. almond extract
2 1/2 c. flour

1/2 t. baking powder
1/4 t. salt
1/3 c. raspberry jam or
   preserves

Preheat oven to 350 degrees. Beat butter and sugar with an electric mixer until light and fluffy. Beat in egg and almond extract. Add flour, baking powder and salt; beat until well blended. Spread in an ungreased 9" square pan. Smooth the surface; using a wet finger, make 5 to 7 diagonal indentations. Fill with jam or preserves. Bake 12 minutes or just until edges are golden brown. Cool; then cut into 1 1/2" squares. Makes 3 dozen.

Apple Oatmeal Bars

Joy Kinnear

1 c. flour
1/2 t. salt
1/2 t. soda
1/2 c. brown sugar
2 T. butter or margarine

1 c. uncooked oatmeal
1/2 c. shortening
3 medium red apples, sliced
1/2 c. granulated sugar

Mix sifted flour, salt and soda with brown sugar. Add oatmeal. Cut in shortening until crumbly. Spread half of mixture in greased baking dish (approximately 11"x7"). Arrange sliced apples over mixture in baking dish, dot with butter and sprinkle with granulated sugar. Cover with remainder of mixture and press firm. Bake at 350 degrees for 45 minutes.

Several years ago, I purchased one of Gooseberry Patch's gnome cookie cutters. Now each cookie plate I make for friends, family and co-workers gets a gnome sugar cookie for "good luck."

Kara Lynn Kimerline

Carrot Cookies

Joy Kinnear

2/3 c. shortening
1 c. granulated sugar or
   firmly packed
   brown sugar
2 eggs
1/2 c. sour milk
1 t. vanilla extract
2 c. rolled oats, uncooked
2 c. flour, sifted

1 t. baking powder
1/2 t. baking soda
1/2 t. salt
1 t. cinnamon
1/2 t. nutmeg
1/2 t. cloves
1/2 c. raisins
1 1/2 c. raw carrots,
   grated finely

Cream shortening and sugar; beat in eggs. Add sour milk and vanilla. Sift dry ingredients together and add the oats. Add flour mixture, raisins and carrots to shortening mixture, a little at a time; stir well. Drop dough in small balls from the top of a spoon onto greased baking sheet. Bake at 375 degrees for 12 to 15 minutes. Makes 4 dozen.

When our daughter was married, we had the wedding reception in our church hall and the family did all the decorating, favors and table centerpieces. We needed something different and special and came up with using the cookie cutters we purchased from Gooseberry Patch. Three of us rolled cookies for a week. On each table we placed a large, white wicker basket lined with cranberry and white tulle. Around and over each basket and handle we wove floral paper ribbon. We placed four dozen sugar cookies in three different heart-shaped sizes in each basket. Standing in the middle of each basket we arranged two heart in hand shaped cookies and placed two golden rings over the middle finger of each cookie. As you can imagine, they were quite a hit!

Nancy Hutchins

Peppermint Pieces

Eleanor Miller

This recipe has been a family favorite for many holiday seasons. They "mysteriously" disappear very rapidly. Often I find an empty container in the refrigerator because no one wants to admit their guilt!

1/2 c. margarine (or butter, if preferred)
2 c. sifted powdered sugar
4 squares unsweetened chocolate, melted

4 eggs
2 t. vanilla
2 t. peppermint flavoring
1 c. vanilla wafer crumbs

Cream butter and sugar until light and fluffy. Add melted chocolate gradually. Add eggs, one at a time, beating after each addition. Add vanilla and peppermint. Sprinkle 1/2 the crumbs in 24 small cupcake liners. Add filling, top with remaining crumbs. Freeze until firm. Serve frozen or cold. This can also be made in a small flat baking dish (11"x7" or 9"x9") and cut into small pieces.

One of my all-time favorite family traditions is "Cookie Day", which we hold on a Sunday in early December. My sisters and I gather together at my mom's kitchen (mom is there too, of course) and bake cookies from dawn until way past dinner. We put some Christmas records on the old turntable and we sing along as we mix, bake and decorate. We end up with several batches of our favorites and divide them up to be used for office cookie exchanges, gift giving and open houses. It's always a fun day and we all look forward to it, as we know it's going to be a day full of laughter and sharing...and of course, sampling!

Cathy Marcquenski

Hoosier Peanut Bars

Eleanor Miller

This recipe belonged to my mother. She always made these bars to take to gatherings, as everyone looked forward to them. When our children were growing up, they always asked for them too!

1/2 c. shortening (margarine)
1/2 c. sugar
1 1/2 c. firmly packed light
    brown sugar
2 eggs
1 t. vanilla
3 T. cold water
6 oz. semi-sweet
    chocolate chips

2 egg whites
3/4 c. chopped salted
    peanuts
1 1/2 c. flour
1 t. baking powder
1/2 t. baking soda
1/2 t. salt

Beat together the shortening, sugar and 1/2 cup brown sugar. Reserve the remaining 1 cup brown sugar for the topping. Blend in 2 eggs and the vanilla. Add the cold water alternately with the sifted dry ingredients. The dough will be stiff. Press dough into a 13"x 9" pan. Sprinkle chocolate chips over the dough and press gently. Beat egg whites until foamy. Gradually add the remaining 1 cup brown sugar and beat until stiff. Spread over chocolate chips. Top with salted peanuts. Press gently. Bake in 325 degree oven for 35 to 40 minutes. Cut into squares while warm.

Double Peanut Butter Cookies

Jean Shaffer

1/4 c. butter or margarine
1/4 c. shortening
1/2 c. peanut butter
1/2 c. granulated sugar
1/2 c. packed brown sugar
1 egg

1 1/4 c. flour
3/4 t. baking soda
1/2 t. baking powder
1/4 t. salt
pkg. peanut butter
    chips

Cream butter or margarine, shortening, peanut butter, both sugars and egg in a large bowl. Blend in dry ingredients. Stir in peanut butter chips. Shape into 1" balls. Flatten in a criss-cross pattern with fork dipped in sugar. Bake at 375 degrees for 10 to 12 minutes or until set. Cool on cookie sheet before moving to wire rack.

★ ☆   ☆

Peanut Butter Cookies with Icing

Charlotte Crockett

For this recipe I use chocolate icing the most, simply because it is everyone's favorite. However, I have changed the icing to butter cream or plain white with different food colorings for the occasion. An example would be Valentine's Day and Christmas. Use the white icing with red food coloring for the top and cinnamon candy; or for St. Patrick's Day do the same except use green food coloring. The combinations are endless and the kids will love it.

1/2 c. shortening (butter-flavored is great)	1 egg
	1/2 t. vanilla
1/2 c. peanut butter	2 c. plus 2 T. flour
1/2 c. granulated sugar	1/2 t. soda
1/2 c. light brown sugar	1/2 t. salt

Cream shortening with peanut butter and both sugars. Add egg and vanilla and beat until light and fluffy. Sift flour, salt and soda over creamed mixture and blend together completely. Form into 1" balls. Place on a greased baking sheet. Press flat with a fork crossways. Bake in a 350 degree oven for 12 to 15 minutes. Makes 3 dozen.

Icing:

1 c. semi-sweet or milk chocolate morsels
1/2 t. shortening or vegetable oil
1 c. chopped pecans or cashews (optional)

Melt together chocolate morsels and oil on top of double boiler. Stir until blended and smooth but do not allow to boil. Or, place in a microwave-safe dish and melt for one minute on high; stir until smooth. Place one teaspoon of melted chocolate on the cooled cookies where the fork made an indentation and spread around. Sprinkle a few chopped nuts on top. When completely cooled and chocolate has hardened, place in an airtight container.

I found an interesting way to decorate peanut butter cookies. Instead of the criss-cross of a fork on top, I looked around my kitchen one day and found that the bottom of a little antique dessert glass had an interesting fluted pattern. I use it now to press on the cookies before baking for a lovely, festive design.

Carol Kirkland

My Favorite Sugar Cookies

Rebecca Suiter

Recently I retired from teaching school and being a school counselor for 27 years. One of my favorite activities was a class birthday party at the end of each month for all the students who were born during that month. The party was always looked forward to with great anticipation. I made each one of the birthday students a paper birthday crown and served punch and cookies. The cookies were always cut-out cookies made from my favorite recipe and cut in the shapes of the season or holiday. This is how my cookie cutter collection was started. I decorated the cookies according to how much time I had, and the cookies I think my students liked the best were the gingerbread men. When I presented them to my students, usually after reading the story **The Gingerbread Man,** I would ask them to hide their eyes, with their heads on their desk, and tell them that we were having a special visitor that day. I placed a decorated cookie on each student's desk and then told them to open their eyes. The expression on each face was worth all the work. Some gobbled up the cookies immediately, but many gazed affectionately at the cookie and saved it to take home and show mother or give to a little brother or sister. Many of my students had never made cut-out cookies, so one of our projects before Christmas was always to make them in the classroom, and the experience provided an opportunity to study measuring and fractions. This was always the highlight of the year. The following is my favorite cookie recipe, because being such a busy person, I never felt I had time to chill the dough before rolling the cookies out. You do not have to chill the dough in this recipe.

3 c. sifted flour	1 c. butter-flavored shortening
1/2 t. baking powder	2 eggs
1/2 t. baking soda	1 c. sugar

Into a bowl, sift together flour, baking powder and baking soda. Cut in shortening as for pie crust. Beat eggs, add sugar and beat well. Blend egg mixture into flour mixture. Roll out to 1/8" thickness on floured board. Cut and lift with spatula to ungreased cookie sheets. Bake in preheated 375 degree oven for 6 to 8 minutes. Remove at once to cooling rack. You can sprinkle sugar on them before baking, if desired. After cooled, decorate with colored frostings.

For as long as I can remember, we always had a large "pull out all the stops" party on Christmas Day. Part of the excitement was the cookie baking my mother would start in November, then wrap and freeze until Christmas. We would average about 18 different types every year; some simple, some more complex, and some true works of art. As the years went on, some of the cookies were deleted, many favorites were repeated, and new "members" continuously joined the family of sweets. My sisters and I would wait patiently as we got closer to the holidays, hoping to take part in the unveiling of these culinary jewels. I was always lucky enough to help my grandfather take each of the carefully wrapped packages out of the freezer to arrange on the crystal and porcelain platters on the dessert table. This table averaged about 5 to 6 feet in length! My grandparents have since passed away, but I was always lucky enough to help my grandfather arrange those trays of cookies on Christmas Eve. We don't have those Christmases at home anymore...they're at my brother's house now, but Mom still bakes cookies for all to enjoy. With each bite, I can still recall the bittersweet memories of those wonderful Christmases at home.

Carol Surowiec

Whoopie Pies

Rebecca Suiter

4 c. sifted flour
2 c. white sugar
1 c shortening
1 c. cocoa
2 t. soda

1 t. salt
2 t. vanilla
2 eggs
1 c. sour milk
1 c. hot water

Mix and drop the above mixture with a large tablespoon onto an ungreased cookie sheet. Bake at 400 degrees for 8 minutes. Cool and sandwich together with filling.

Filling:

2 egg whites, beaten
2 T. vanilla
4 T. flour

4 T. milk
2 c. powdered sugar
1/2 c. shortening

Beat shortening and powdered sugar. Add flour, vanilla and milk. Fold in beaten egg whites.

Cookie Cutter Cutting Boards

Trace a cookie cutter on a piece of plain paper. Enlarge the drawing. Cut this enlarged picture out of wood, stain and then varnish. Make cookies in the same shape or a loaf of holiday bread. Place on the board, cover with clear cellophane and tie with a festive ribbon. Can be used as a simple cutting board or just for decoration.

Connie Himmelberger

Lemon Snowdrops

Pat Habiger

1 c. butter
1/2 c. confectioner's sugar
1 t. lemon extract
2 c. flour
1/4 t. salt

1 egg, slightly beaten
grated rind of 1 lemon
2/3 c. sugar
3 T. lemon juice
1 1/2 T. softened butter

Cream together butter and sugar, add extract. Sift flour and salt together; add to creamed mixture, mixing well. Using level tea-spoons of dough, form balls. Flatten slightly. Place 1" apart on ungreased baking sheet. Bake at 350 degrees for 8 to 10 min-utes. Let cool. Make lemon butter filling by combining beaten egg, rind, sugar, lemon juice, and butter in top of double boiler. Cook over hot water until thick, stirring constantly. Let cool. Put two cookies together with filling between. Roll in confectioner's sugar. Makes 2 1/2 to 3 dozen cookies.

Lemon-Iced Apple Jelly Cookies

Gary Oldenburg

1 c. butter or margarine,
    softened
3/4 c. sugar

1/2 c. apple jelly
1 t. vanilla
3 c. flour

Cream butter and sugar in a large bowl until fluffy. Add jelly and vanilla; blend well. Add flour; mix until a soft dough forms. Cover and chill at least 30 minutes. Preheat oven to 300 degrees. On a lightly floured surface use a floured rolling pin to roll out dough to 1/4" thickness. Cut out cookies; transfer to a greased baking sheet. Bake 20 to 25 minutes, or until cookies are light brown. Cool on a wire rack. Ice.

Icing:

4 1/2 c. powdered sugar, sifted
3/4 c. milk
1 t. lemon extract

Stir powdered sugar, milk and lemon extract together in a large bowl until smooth. Ice cooled cookies; allow icing to harden before storing in an airtight container. Yield: About 4 dozen 3" cookies.

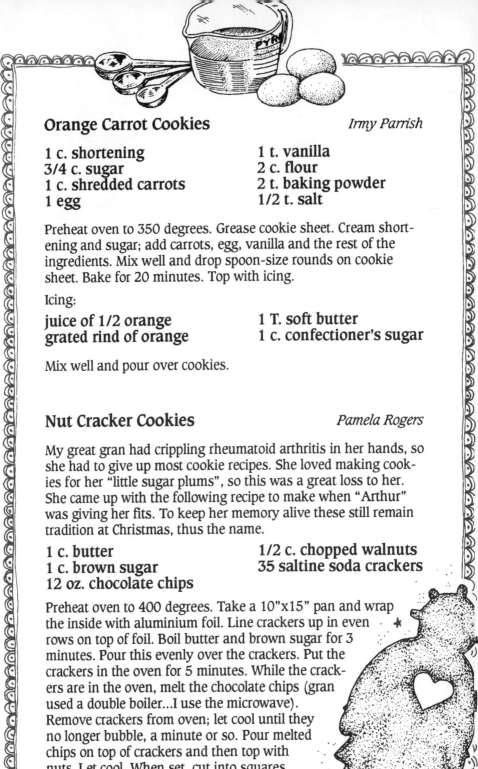

Orange Carrot Cookies

Irmy Parrish

1 c. shortening
3/4 c. sugar
1 c. shredded carrots
1 egg

1 t. vanilla
2 c. flour
2 t. baking powder
1/2 t. salt

Preheat oven to 350 degrees. Grease cookie sheet. Cream shortening and sugar; add carrots, egg, vanilla and the rest of the ingredients. Mix well and drop spoon-size rounds on cookie sheet. Bake for 20 minutes. Top with icing.

Icing:

juice of 1/2 orange
grated rind of orange

1 T. soft butter
1 c. confectioner's sugar

Mix well and pour over cookies.

Nut Cracker Cookies

Pamela Rogers

My great gran had crippling rheumatoid arthritis in her hands, so she had to give up most cookie recipes. She loved making cookies for her "little sugar plums", so this was a great loss to her. She came up with the following recipe to make when "Arthur" was giving her fits. To keep her memory alive these still remain tradition at Christmas, thus the name.

1 c. butter
1 c. brown sugar
12 oz. chocolate chips

1/2 c. chopped walnuts
35 saltine soda crackers

Preheat oven to 400 degrees. Take a 10"x15" pan and wrap the inside with aluminium foil. Line crackers up in even rows on top of foil. Boil butter and brown sugar for 3 minutes. Pour this evenly over the crackers. Put the crackers in the oven for 5 minutes. While the crackers are in the oven, melt the chocolate chips (gran used a double boiler...I use the microwave). Remove crackers from oven; let cool until they no longer bubble, a minute or so. Pour melted chips on top of crackers and then top with nuts. Let cool. When set, cut into squares.

I Love Shortbread

Sally McArthur

3/4 c. butter, softened (margarine not recommended)
1/4 c. sugar

1 3/4 c. all-purpose flour
dash of salt
powdered sugar

Mix together butter and sugar. Stir in flour and salt. Mixture will be dry and crumbly. With clean hands, pinch mixture together until it all sticks together. Shape dough into a ball. Sprinkle clean work surface (such as a kitchen counter) with flour. Place dough on surface and roll dough out to a 1/4" thickness. Cut out with favorite shape cookie cutter. Place 2 1/2" apart on cookie sheet and bake at 350 degrees until golden brown on edges (about 10 to 15 minutes). Place powdered sugar into a shaker and dust over each cookie to lightly cover.

Vanilla Sugar

Grace Meletta

2 vanilla beans

2 c. granulated sugar

Place vanilla beans in jar. Cover completely with sugar; cover jar tightly. Store in cool place for 2 weeks, to be used in any cookie recipe. Wonderful taste. Not to be used in place of vanilla extract in your recipes.

At Christmas my children always offered my service for providing cookies for their class parties. I worked two jobs and time was valuable, so I would buy box cookies in Christmasy shapes and decorate with icing (red, green and white), colored sugars, bits of licorice and gumdrops. Easy way to do your duty!

Charlene Robedee

Caramel Filled Chocolate Cookies

Vicki Belles

2 1/4 c. flour
3/4 c. cocoa
1 t. baking soda
1 c. white sugar plus
   1 T., set aside
1 c. brown sugar

1 c. margarine
2 t. vanilla
2 eggs
1 c. chopped pecans, divided
48 chocolate covered
   caramels

Combine 1 tablespoon sugar and 1/2 of the nuts; set aside. Combine dry ingredients; set aside. In a medium mixing bowl, cream sugars and margarine until fluffy. Add eggs and vanilla. Stir in flour mixture plus the other 1/2 cup nuts. For each cookie, shape 1 tablespoon of dough around one candy. Dip the dough ball, one side only, into the sugar/nut mixture. Bake the cookies on an ungreased cookie sheet, sugar/nut mixture side up. Bake at 375 degrees for 7 to 10 minutes. Cool cookies for 2 minutes before removing them from the cookie sheet onto wire racks to finish cooling. Yield: 4 dozen.

Buckeyes

Michele U'Sellis

1/4 lb. butter
3 c. crispy rice cereal,
   finely chopped
1 lb. confectioner's sugar

12 oz. chocolate chips
1/2 stick paraffin wax
2 c. peanut butter

Melt butter and mix with peanut butter. Add sugar and cereal to peanut butter/butter mixture. With hands form small balls. Melt chocolate chips and paraffin wax in a separate pan. With the help of a toothpick, dip balls in chocolate mixture. Cool on waxed paper.

Overmixing dough can cause tough cookies.
For tender cookies, mix ingredients just until
combined, unless recipe specifies otherwise.

Michele Urdahl

Pecan Chocolate Chip Bars

Judy Conn

This yummy, chewy version resembles a classic chocolate chip cookie baked in bar form.

1 3/4 c. flour
1/2 t. salt
1 c. butter, softened
1 1/2 c. light brown sugar
1 t. vanilla

2 eggs
2 c. chocolate chips,
  divided
1 1/2 c. coarsely chopped
  pecans, divided

In a small bowl combine flour and salt. In mixer bowl cream butter and sugar until light and fluffy. Beat in vanilla. Add eggs, one at a time, beating well after each addition. Gradually beat in flour. Stir in 1 1/2 cups of chocolate chips and 3/4 cup of pecans. Spread into greased 15 1/2"x10 1/2" jelly roll pan. Sprinkle with remaining 1/2 cup chocolate chips and 3/4 cup of pecans. Bake at 375 degrees for 25 minutes. Cool, then cut into 2 1/2"x1 1/2" bars. Makes 24 bars. Store in airtight container.

Caramel Candy Bar Cookie

Janet Heberer

1 c. flour
1 c. oatmeal
1/2 t. soda
3/4 c. butter or margarine
3/4 c. sugar
14 oz. pkg. caramels

1/3 c. evaporated milk
1/2 c. chopped nuts
1 c. butterscotch or
  semi-sweet chocolate
  pieces

Combine flour, oats and baking soda. In mixing bowl, beat butter or margarine for 30 seconds. Add sugar and beat until fluffy. Beat in oat mixture until crumbly. Do not overmix. Reserve 1 cup of crust mixture. Press the remaining mixture onto bottom of 13"x9"x2" baking pan. Bake the crust layer at 350 degrees for 10 minutes. Cool in pan for 10 minutes. Meanwhile, in a saucepan cook the caramels and milk over low heat until the caramels melt and the mixture is smooth. Spread over pre-baked crust. Sprinkle with nuts and then with the reserved crumbs and chips. Bake at 350 degrees for 15 to 20 minutes or until top crumbs turn golden. Cool in pan. Cut into bars. Makes 32 cookies.

Peach Cookies

Edwina Gadsby

It's fun to watch people's reaction when they see these cookies...they're not quite sure what they are at first. They look like miniature peaches and taste delicious!

3/4 c. unsalted butter, softened
1/2 c. milk
1 c. granulated sugar
2 eggs
1 t. baking powder
3 3/4 c. all-purpose flour
1 t. vanilla
2/3 c. apricot jam
2 t. apricot brandy
1/4 c. semi-sweet chocolate pieces, melted
1/3 c. ground pecans
1/4 c. water
1/3 c. red sugar*
2/3 c. yellow-orange sugar*
whole cloves and edible leaves for garnish (optional)

In the bowl of an electric mixer, combine butter, milk, sugar, eggs, baking powder and 2 cups of flour. Beat on medium speed until well mixed. Stir in remaining 1 3/4 cup flour and vanilla. Mix until dough is smooth. Shape dough into smooth 3/4" balls (each ball is half of a peach). Place 1" apart on an ungreased baking sheet. Bake at 325 degrees until cookies are brown on the bottom (about 15 to 20 minutes). Cool on wire racks. Place the tip of a small knife on the center of the flat side of each cookie and hollow out. Reserve crumbs that fall out. Mix 1 1/2 cups of cookie crumbs with jam, chocolate, nuts and brandy. Fill the hollowed cookies with the crumb mixture to make a "pit". Set 2 filled cookies, flat sides together to form "peach". Press together gently. Brush each "peach" lightly with water. Immediately roll one side of the "peach" in red sugar for blush. Sprinkle yellow-orange sugar on the "peach" to cover completely. Insert whole clove at top for stem and garnish with leaves, if desired. Set aside to dry. Makes 4 dozen. *To color sugar: Place granulated sugar in heavy-duty plastic bag with zip-lock top. For red: Sprinkle 3 drops of red liquid food color over sugar. Seal top of bag and toss to color sugar. For yellow-orange: Sprinkle 4 drops of yellow liquid food color and 2 drops of red liquid food color over sugar. Repeat steps above.

G&G Cookies

Mary Alice Foster

I was the winner in Crisco's "Smart Cookie" contest. This is my prize winning recipe. I put two or three recipes together and came up with this prize winner. I named the cookies G&G because they are GOOD and GOOD for you. Note the oatmeal, raisins, peanut butter chips, coconut and nuts...like a walking health store. Make, eat, enjoy!

1 1/2 butter-flavored shortening sticks (or 1 1/2 c.)
1 1/2 c. firmly packed brown sugar
3 T. milk
2 eggs
1 1/4 c. all-purpose flour
1 t. baking powder
1/2 t. baking soda
1/2 t. salt
3 c. quick oats (not instant or old-fashioned)
2 1/4 c. raisins
10 oz. pkg. peanut butter chips
1 1/4 c. coconut
1 c. chopped walnuts or pecans

Heat oven to 350 degrees. Combine butter-flavored shortening, brown sugar and milk in a large bowl. Beat at medium speed of electric mixer until well blended. Beat in eggs. Combine flour, baking powder, baking soda and salt. Add to creamed mixture at low speed until just blended. Stir in, one at a time, oats, raisins, peanut butter chips, coconut and nuts with spoon. Form dough into 1 1/2" balls (if dough is too sticky, refrigerate for 1 hour and/or flour or grease fingers for ease in handling). Place balls 2" apart on lightly greased baking sheet. Flatten slightly. Bake at 350 degrees for 10 to 12 minutes, or until set and light golden brown. Do not overbake. Cool on baking sheet for 2 minutes then remove to kitchen counter. Makes about 5 dozen cookies.

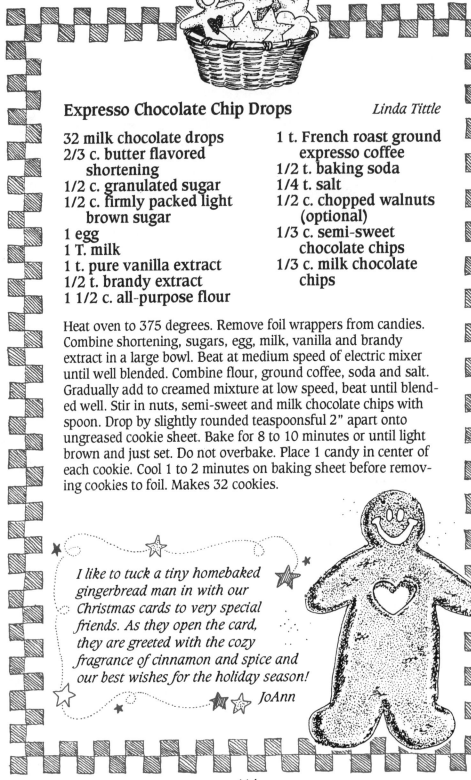

Expresso Chocolate Chip Drops

Linda Tittle

32 milk chocolate drops
2/3 c. butter flavored
    shortening
1/2 c. granulated sugar
1/2 c. firmly packed light
    brown sugar
1 egg
1 T. milk
1 t. pure vanilla extract
1/2 t. brandy extract
1 1/2 c. all-purpose flour

1 t. French roast ground
    expresso coffee
1/2 t. baking soda
1/4 t. salt
1/2 c. chopped walnuts
    (optional)
1/3 c. semi-sweet
    chocolate chips
1/3 c. milk chocolate
    chips

Heat oven to 375 degrees. Remove foil wrappers from candies. Combine shortening, sugars, egg, milk, vanilla and brandy extract in a large bowl. Beat at medium speed of electric mixer until well blended. Combine flour, ground coffee, soda and salt. Gradually add to creamed mixture at low speed, beat until blended well. Stir in nuts, semi-sweet and milk chocolate chips with spoon. Drop by slightly rounded teaspoonsful 2" apart onto ungreased cookie sheet. Bake for 8 to 10 minutes or until light brown and just set. Do not overbake. Place 1 candy in center of each cookie. Cool 1 to 2 minutes on baking sheet before removing cookies to foil. Makes 32 cookies.

I like to tuck a tiny homebaked gingerbread man in with our Christmas cards to very special friends. As they open the card, they are greeted with the cozy fragrance of cinnamon and spice and our best wishes for the holiday season!

JoAnn

Orange Drop Cookies

Judy Martin

A blue ribbon winner at the county fair!

1/2 c. shortening	2 1/2 c. flour
1 c. sugar	1/2 t. salt
2 eggs	1 T. grated orange peel
1/2 c. orange juice	1/2 c. nuts
1 1/2 t. baking powder	

Cream together shortening and sugar; add eggs one at a time, and beat well. Add orange juice and mix. Blend in dry ingredients. Drop onto cookie sheet. Bake at 350 degrees for 10 minutes.

Orange Frosting:

6 T. butter
2 t. grated orange peel
1 lb. bag confectioner's
    sugar
2 T. orange juice
1 1/2 t. vanilla

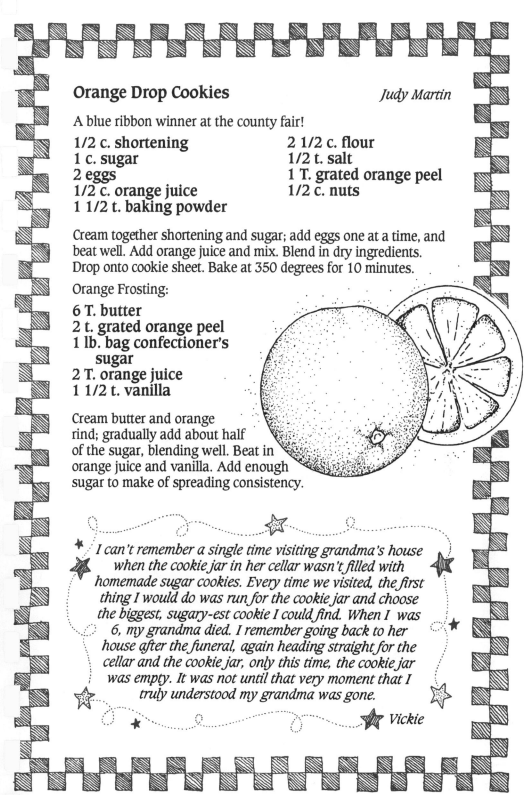

Cream butter and orange rind; gradually add about half of the sugar, blending well. Beat in orange juice and vanilla. Add enough sugar to make of spreading consistency.

I can't remember a single time visiting grandma's house when the cookie jar in her cellar wasn't filled with homemade sugar cookies. Every time we visited, the first thing I would do was run for the cookie jar and choose the biggest, sugary-est cookie I could find. When I was 6, my grandma died. I remember going back to her house after the funeral, again heading straight for the cellar and the cookie jar, only this time, the cookie jar was empty. It was not until that very moment that I truly understood my grandma was gone.

Vickie

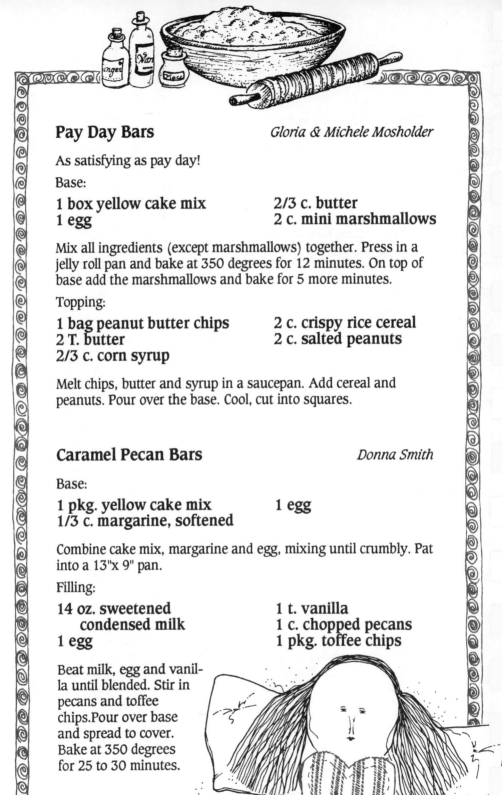

Pay Day Bars

Gloria & Michele Mosholder

As satisfying as pay day!

Base:

1 box yellow cake mix	2/3 c. butter
1 egg	2 c. mini marshmallows

Mix all ingredients (except marshmallows) together. Press in a jelly roll pan and bake at 350 degrees for 12 minutes. On top of base add the marshmallows and bake for 5 more minutes.

Topping:

1 bag peanut butter chips	2 c. crispy rice cereal
2 T. butter	2 c. salted peanuts
2/3 c. corn syrup	

Melt chips, butter and syrup in a saucepan. Add cereal and peanuts. Pour over the base. Cool, cut into squares.

Caramel Pecan Bars

Donna Smith

Base:

1 pkg. yellow cake mix	1 egg
1/3 c. margarine, softened	

Combine cake mix, margarine and egg, mixing until crumbly. Pat into a 13"x 9" pan.

Filling:

14 oz. sweetened condensed milk	1 t. vanilla
	1 c. chopped pecans
1 egg	1 pkg. toffee chips

Beat milk, egg and vanilla until blended. Stir in pecans and toffee chips. Pour over base and spread to cover. Bake at 350 degrees for 25 to 30 minutes.

Chocolate Sandwich Cookie Bark

Karla Nitz

1 lb. almond bark, melted
5 chocolate sandwich cookies
nuts, or crushed pastel party mints (optional)

Use a knife to cut cookies (if they crumble too much, the bark ends up looking "dirty"). After melting almond bark, add cookies (and nuts or crushed mints). Spread thinly on aluminum foil. Cool until hardened and break into pieces. Bark can be colored pink or green by adding paste food coloring to bark as it is melted.

I proposed the idea of a Cookie Walk and our church council approved the project. Here's how it works. Each lady in our church is asked to bake 3 batches of her favorite, finest Christmas cookies. On the day of the Cookie Walk, two very long tables are lined with tray after tray of wonderful, delicious, beautiful cookies. Customers, when entering, receive an empty 2-lb. bakery box and one glove that they wear so they don't actually touch any of the cookies. When they are done choosing, we weigh the cookies and charge by the pound. Our goal...to make someone else's Christmas who is less fortunate, a little bit better.

Jeanne Kenna

117

Peanut Blossoms

Chris Montgomery

I had just finished college and was on a limited budget, but wanted to do something special for my youth group. So I rushed to the grocery store to buy cookie ingredients and milk chocolate drops for one of my favorite recipes. I busied myself mixing up a double batch and baking the yummy cookies, knowing that the kids would love this special treat. My roommate came home and asked to sample one. "Sure," I said, "there will be lots so help yourself." She chose a cookie and left. In a minute she returned and asked, "Have you eaten one yet?" "No," I replied, "I can't eat any until I'm done baking them or I'll keep eating them." She insisted that I try one, so I gave in and took a big bite of one, knowing that I would thoroughly enjoy it. To the wastebasket I ran. It tasted awful! After discussing what it tasted like we found the problem...my roommate had placed salt in the extra sugar container. What an "insalt" to my special treat!

1/2 c. shortening	1 3/4 c. flour
1/2 c. peanut butter	1 t. soda
1/2 c. brown sugar	1/2 t. salt
1/2 c. white sugar	milk chocolate drops or
1 egg	chocolate star candies
1 t. vanilla	

Cream together the shortening, peanut butter and sugars. Add the egg and vanilla. Sift together the flour, soda and salt; add to creamed mixture. Shape dough into balls the size of a walnut.

Roll in sugar. Place on an ungreased cookie sheet and bake at 375 degrees for 10 minutes. Remove from oven. Remove foil wrappers from milk chocolate drops. Top each cookie with a drop or star, pressing firmly into the center of cookie.

Cookies will crack. Bake 2 to 5 minutes longer.

Double panning cookie sheets (stack one on top of the other) can prevent cookies from burning on the bottom.

Michele Urdahl

118

Halloween Cookie Pizza

Sandie Voss

I make the Halloween Pizza every year to take to work on Halloween. It is so popular that this year I made two cookie pizzas so they would last until break time!

3/4 c. packed light
   brown sugar
1/2 c. margarine
1 egg
1 T. water
1 t. vanilla extract
1 1/4 c. all-purpose flour

1/2 t. baking soda
1/4 t. salt
1 c. peanut butter chips
1 c. miniature marshmallows
1/2 c. semi-sweet
   chocolate chips
1/2 c. chopped pecans

Preheat oven to 350 degrees. Lightly grease a 12" pizza pan. In a large mixer bowl beat sugar and margarine until creamy. Add egg, water and vanilla; beat well. In a separate bowl, stir together flour, baking soda and salt; add to sugar mixture, beating on low speed until blended. Stir in peanut butter chips. Spread batter in prepared pan to within 1/2" of the edge. Bake 11 to 13 minutes or until set. Remove from oven. Sprinkle marshmallows, chocolate chips and pecans over top. Return to oven. Bake 5 to 7 minutes or until marshmallows are lightly browned. Cool completely. Blend chocolate drizzle ingredients and melt; drizzle over top.

Chocolate Drizzle:

1/4 c. semi-sweet chocolate chips
2 to 3 t. margarine

Blend orange drizzle ingredients and drizzle over chocolate.

Orange Drizzle:

1/2 c. powdered sugar
1 T. water
3 drops yellow food
   coloring
2 drops red food
   coloring

Let stand about
1 hour until
drizzle sets.

German Chocolate Cake Mix Cookies

Ann Fehr

1 pkg. German
    chocolate cake mix
1 c. semi-sweet
    chocolate chips

1/2 c. rolled oats
1/2 c. raisins
1/2 c. oil
2 eggs, slightly beaten

Heat oven to 350 degrees. In a large bowl combine all the ingredients, blending well. Drop dough by rounded teaspoonsful 2" apart onto ungreased cookie sheets. Bake for 8 to 10 minutes or until set. Cool for 1 minute and remove from cookie sheets. Makes 4 1/2 dozen cookies.

Toffee Bars

Delores Berg

15 graham crackers
1 c. brown sugar
1 c. butter

6 oz. chocolate or
    butterscotch chips
1/4 c. chopped walnuts,
    pecans or slivered almonds

Heavily grease cookie sheet. Arrange crackers over sheet. In a saucepan combine sugar and butter, bring to a boil. Pour over crackers. Bake at 400 degrees for 5 minutes. Sprinkle with chocolate chips. Spread when soft. Sprinkle with nuts. Chill. Cut or break into pieces.

People always ask me how I get my cookies
so moist and chewy. Simple,
DO NOT OVER BAKE!

Candy Hannigan

Frosted Maple Cookies

Denise Green

1 c. raisins
3/4 c. water
2 3/4 c. sifted flour
2 1/3 t. maple flavoring
1/2 c. butter

1 1/2 c. powdered sugar
2 eggs
1/4 t. salt
1 t. baking soda

Cook raisins in water until enough liquid remains to measure 1/2 cup; add baking soda. In a separate bowl cream butter and powdered sugar, add eggs and blend. Add the flour, salt and maple flavoring; then add the raisins. Cool mixture in refrigerator for 2 hours before baking. Drop by teaspoonsful on greased cookie sheet. Bake at 350 degrees for 12 to 15 minutes.

Maple Cream Frosting:

1/4 c. butter
1 3/4 c. powdered sugar

2 T. cream
1 t. maple flavoring

Cream butter, sugar, cream and flavoring. Spread on top of cookies.

Hamburger Cookies

Cynthia Anderson

1 box vanilla wafers
1 box chocolate covered cookies (the same size
    as the wafers)
1 can vanilla icing
1 bag coconut
sesame seeds
light corn syrup
green food coloring

Color coconut with green food coloring and set aside. Ice bottom of vanilla wafer. Sprinkle with coconut close to the edges. Add chocolate covered cookie. Ice over chocolate cookie. Top with vanilla wafer.
Brush top lightly with corn syrup. Sprinkle on sesame seeds.

Banana Spice Cookies

Denise Green

1/2 c. shortening
1/4 t. salt
2 c. flour
1 c. brown sugar
1/4 t. cloves
1/4 t. baking soda

1 c. mashed banana
1/4 c. softened butter
1/2 t. cinnamon
2 t. baking powder
2 eggs
1/2 c. chopped nuts

Mix together shortening, butter, brown sugar, eggs and banana. Stir in remaining ingredients. Cover; chill for about 1 hour. Drop by rounded teaspoonful onto greased cookie sheet. Bake at 375 degrees for 8 to 10 minutes; let cool. Prepare Browned Butter Icing and spread over cookies.

Browned Butter Icing:

1/3 c. butter
3 c. powdered sugar

2 T. milk
1 1/2 t. vanilla

In a saucepan brown butter over medium heat until delicately browned. Stir in powdered sugar, milk and vanilla; beat until smooth and of spreading consistency. Makes about 3 1/2 dozen.

Sunflower Sugar Cookies

Delores Berg

3/4 c. sugar
1 egg, beaten
2 c. flour
1/2 c. shortening
1/2 c. butter or butter
   flavored shortening

1/2 t. baking soda
1 t. cream of tartar
1 c. sunflower seeds
2 t. vanilla

Mix and roll into balls. Press with sugared bottom of a glass to slightly flatten. Bake at 375 degrees for 10 minutes.

Grandma's Orange-Carrot Cookies *Heather Hood*

This recipe was passed down from my grandmother who was famous for these cookies. They were often given as gifts and were always considered a special treat.

2/3 c. shortening
1 c. sugar
1 egg, beaten
2 1/2 c. flour
1 c. carrots, cooked and coarsely
    mashed (about 4 large carrots)
3 T. freshly squeezed orange
    juice with rind

2 t. baking powder
1/4 t. salt
1 t. vanilla

Mix together shortening, sugar and egg. Sift together flour, baking powder and salt; add to shortening mixture. Add carrots, orange juice/rind, and vanilla. Drop by teaspoonsful onto cookie sheet. Bake at 375 degrees for 10 to 12 minutes. Top with icing. Makes about four dozen.

Icing:

2 c. powdered sugar
2 T. butter
1/4 c. freshly squeezed orange juice
    with rind

Blend ingredients until smooth,
top cookies when cool.

★ ☆ ★ ☆ ★

Cookie Coupon

Purchase ten stamped postcards at the post office.
Print your address on the front of each card. On the back of each card make a cookie coupon saying: Good for at least two (2) dozen whatever cookie you wish to bake. Make a checklist that the recipient can check showing whether they would like nuts or not, raisins or not (whatever you would like to include in the cookies). At the bottom of the coupon, print: To arrive within ten (10) days.

Shirley Baker

Orange Teacake Cookies

Joy Torkelson

One of my earliest memories of my Grandma Lee and her kitchen is the taste and smell of her "Orange Teacakes". A buttery, yummy, orange-flavored sugar cookie recipe. Grandma always made them with a 5 1/2" or 4" round, scalloped cookie cutter. She used to smile as she handed her small grandchildren these favorite treats, saying, "These are two-handed cookies!" She loved to see a child's two chubby hands hold one of her Orange Teacakes. Grandma hid her mouthwatering treasures in a clear glass gallon jar with a green lid, in the back of a lower kitchen cupboard...as my cousins and I knew well! Grandma was so good at pretending she wasn't aware that we were "snitching" cookies. And she laughingly accepted the sugary cookie kisses of her little culprits and never scolded when she would find our trail of cookie crumbs. I grew up on these Orange Teacake Cookies. This recipe and my cookie jar are all I have of my grandma...but oh, what a legacy!

1 c. butter
1 c. sugar
1 T. grated orange peel
1 T. orange juice

2 t. orange extract
2 eggs
3 c. flour
1 t. baking powder

Cream butter and sugar. Add orange peel, orange juice and orange extract. Then add the eggs, beating well. Sift together flour and baking powder, add to creamed mixture. Refrigerate dough until well chilled. Separate dough into thirds. Roll out 1/3 at a time on floured pastry cloth. Roll thin, cut with cookie cutters and place on greased cookie sheet. Sprinkle with sugar. Bake at 350 degrees for about 8 minutes.

Whenever I bake any cookie, I always use a cooled cookie sheet and I rinse my cookie sheets after every batch to cool the pan down and to remove any residue. My cookie sheets stay shiny and do not turn black. Shiny cookie sheets bake the cookies evenly.

Pat Akers

Lemon Coconut Date Bars

Ann Fehr

1 c. flour
1/4 lb. butter
1/4 c. powdered sugar
2 eggs, beaten
1/2 c. granulated sugar

1 pkg. lemon pudding &
 pie filling
1/2 t. baking powder
1/2 c. chopped dates
1 c. coconut

Cream butter and powdered sugar, add flour. Spread in an 8"x8" pan. Bake at 350 degrees for 15 to 20 minutes. Combine eggs, granulated sugar, lemon pie mix, baking powder, dates and coconut. Spread on hot dough. Bake for 20 to 25 minutes more. Cut while hot and sprinkle with powdered sugar. Makes 20 cookies.

Using your favorite cut-out cookie recipe, cut out and bake cookies using gingerbread boy and girl shaped cutters. When cool, tie bows around their necks to differentiate between boys and girls using 1/8" wide blue and pink grosgrain ribbon. Faces may be left blank or decorated with decorator icing.

Susan Seman

Make Christmas sugar shakers and sprinkle a little Christmas magic on oatmeal, ice cream and cookies!

Christmas Magic

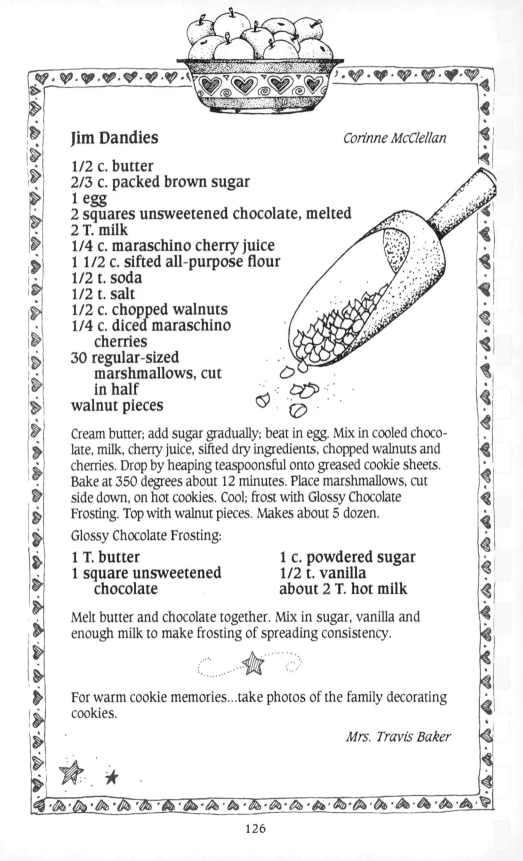

Jim Dandies

Corinne McClellan

1/2 c. butter
2/3 c. packed brown sugar
1 egg
2 squares unsweetened chocolate, melted
2 T. milk
1/4 c. maraschino cherry juice
1 1/2 c. sifted all-purpose flour
1/2 t. soda
1/2 t. salt
1/2 c. chopped walnuts
1/4 c. diced maraschino
   cherries
30 regular-sized
   marshmallows, cut
   in half
walnut pieces

Cream butter; add sugar gradually; beat in egg. Mix in cooled chocolate, milk, cherry juice, sifted dry ingredients, chopped walnuts and
cherries. Drop by heaping teaspoonsful onto greased cookie sheets.
Bake at 350 degrees about 12 minutes. Place marshmallows, cut
side down, on hot cookies. Cool; frost with Glossy Chocolate
Frosting. Top with walnut pieces. Makes about 5 dozen.

Glossy Chocolate Frosting:

1 T. butter
1 square unsweetened
   chocolate

1 c. powdered sugar
1/2 t. vanilla
about 2 T. hot milk

Melt butter and chocolate together. Mix in sugar, vanilla and
enough milk to make frosting of spreading consistency.

For warm cookie memories...take photos of the family decorating
cookies.

Mrs. Travis Baker

126

Sour Cream Cookies

Melissa Bromen

1/2 c. shortening
1 1/2 c. brown sugar
2 eggs
1 c. sour cream
1 t. vanilla

2 3/4 c. flour
1/2 t. baking soda
1/2 t. baking powder
1/2 t. salt
2/3 c. chopped nuts

Mix together thoroughly the shortening, brown sugar and eggs. Stir in sour cream and vanilla. Sift flour, soda, baking powder and salt; stir into sour cream mixture. Add nuts. Chill at least 1 hour. Drop by rounded teaspoonsful about 2" apart on ungreased baking sheet. Bake until delicately browned, about 8 to 10 minutes at 400 degrees. Makes about 5 dozen cookies.

Burnt Butter Icing:

4 T. butter
1 c. sifted powdered sugar

1/2 t. vanilla
1 to 2 T. hot water

Melt butter until golden brown. Blend in powdered sugar and vanilla. Stir in hot water until icing spreads smoothly. Icing for about 30 cookies.

Turkey Cookies

Cynthia Anderson

1 pkg. chocolate sandwich cookies
1 pkg. malted milk balls
1 container red hots
1 bag candy corn
1 can chocolate icing

Split cookies so that white icing is on one side only. Take the plain side, ice with chocolate icing. Place candy corn around edge leaving space at bottom to form tail. Connect tail to cookie with white icing by placing a dollop of chocolate icing on edge. Place malted milk ball against tail back in opening. Dot malted milk ball with chocolate icing. Top with red hot for head.

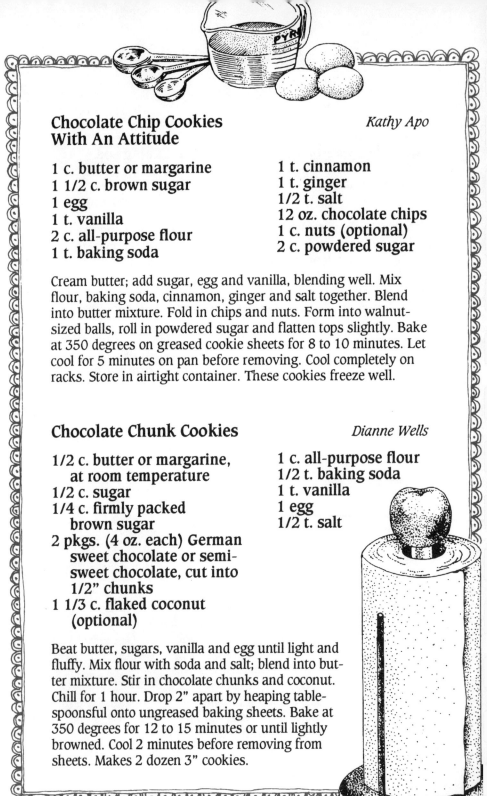

Chocolate Chip Cookies With An Attitude

Kathy Apo

1 c. butter or margarine
1 1/2 c. brown sugar
1 egg
1 t. vanilla
2 c. all-purpose flour
1 t. baking soda

1 t. cinnamon
1 t. ginger
1/2 t. salt
12 oz. chocolate chips
1 c. nuts (optional)
2 c. powdered sugar

Cream butter; add sugar, egg and vanilla, blending well. Mix flour, baking soda, cinnamon, ginger and salt together. Blend into butter mixture. Fold in chips and nuts. Form into walnut-sized balls, roll in powdered sugar and flatten tops slightly. Bake at 350 degrees on greased cookie sheets for 8 to 10 minutes. Let cool for 5 minutes on pan before removing. Cool completely on racks. Store in airtight container. These cookies freeze well.

Chocolate Chunk Cookies

Dianne Wells

1/2 c. butter or margarine,
   at room temperature
1/2 c. sugar
1/4 c. firmly packed
   brown sugar
2 pkgs. (4 oz. each) German
   sweet chocolate or semi-
   sweet chocolate, cut into
   1/2" chunks
1 1/3 c. flaked coconut
   (optional)

1 c. all-purpose flour
1/2 t. baking soda
1 t. vanilla
1 egg
1/2 t. salt

Beat butter, sugars, vanilla and egg until light and fluffy. Mix flour with soda and salt; blend into butter mixture. Stir in chocolate chunks and coconut. Chill for 1 hour. Drop 2" apart by heaping table-spoonsful onto ungreased baking sheets. Bake at 350 degrees for 12 to 15 minutes or until lightly browned. Cool 2 minutes before removing from sheets. Makes 2 dozen 3" cookies.

Mom's Brown Sugar Cookies

Melissa Bromen

1 c. butter	2 c. sifted flour
1/2 c. brown sugar	1 t. salt
1/2 c. granulated sugar	1/2 t. baking soda
1 egg	1/2 c. finely ground nuts
1 t. vanilla	(I usually use walnuts)

Combine ingredients and chill dough for 20 minutes. Shape into small balls, roll in granulated sugar. Place on ungreased cookie sheet. Press flat with bottom of a glass. Bake for 10 to 12 minutes at 350 degrees. Cool and frost. Makes about 7 dozen.

Brown Sugar Icing:

1 c. brown sugar	1 c. sifted powdered sugar
1/2 c. cream	

Boil brown sugar and cream for about 4 minutes. Remove from heat. Beat in powdered sugar.

If crisp cookies soften, heat in 275 to 300 degree oven for 3 to 5 minutes.

Mrs. Travis Baker

A great Christmas gift idea is to decorate a small artificial or live tree with cookie cutters and cookies.

Patricia Husek

My great-grandmother used to put all her sugar cookies into a pillow case and close it with a string. Then she would carry it up to the attic and hang the pillow case on a hook. The cookies always stayed fresh and my mother tells me that they used to taste better when she brought them down for the holidays.

Sharon Scurto

Fruitcake Cookies

Kim Breuer

As an Air Force family, we have lived in four different states over the years and have been fortunate enough to make and keep many good friendships as a result. One of the things I like to do is to collect at least one recipe from new friends and keep it in a special cookbook. This Fruitcake Cookie recipe is one of those recipes. My very good friend gave several dozen of these cookies to us one Christmas, all wrapped so pretty. Of course, we enjoyed the cookies so much, I asked for the recipe and have used it many times since over the years. Because the full recipe makes so many, it was particularly handy one year during a major event for our Air Force B-52 crew member husbands called an Operation Readiness Inspection. We were asked to make and package cookies for the Cookie Bus. Volunteer wives from the Officers' Wives Club would go out on the "bus" and pass out cookies to the aircrew and maintenance crews during their long 12 plus hour shifts. This recipe made more than enough to contribute to the cookie bus. More importantly, though, each time I make it, I think of my wonderful friend. The Air Force brings families together for a few years, and then sends them hither and yon, but the friendships always remain!

1 c. melted margarine
1 c. packed brown sugar
3 eggs
3 c. flour
1 t. baking soda
1 t. cinnamon
7 c. chopped nuts
1/2 c. milk

12 oz. candied pineapple
8 oz. pkg. candied red cherries
8 oz. pkg. candied green cherries
2- 8 oz. pkgs. dates
15 oz. box white raisins

Combine brown sugar and margarine. Add eggs. Combine dry ingredients with milk alternately. Stir fruit and nuts into dough (you may have to use your hands to stir dough at this point because it's VERY stiff). Drop by heaping teaspoonsful onto well-greased cookie sheets and bake at 300 degrees for 20 minutes. Makes about 16 dozen cookies. Excellent for Christmas gift giving or holiday parties as they freeze well. Of course, you may halve the recipe if 16 dozen is too many.

Mother's Cookies

Barbara Loe

My parents made Christmas so very special for their only child, and my memories are extensive and heart-warming. My mother loved to make all kinds of treats in the kitchen. These cookies are my favorites, if I had to choose just one!

1 c. butter
1/2 c. sifted powdered
   sugar
2 t. vanilla
2 c. flour

1/4 t. salt
2 c. pecans, chopped
   very fine
2 c. powdered sugar,
   reserved

Cream butter and 1/2 cup sugar well. Slowly add vanilla, salt; then flour and pecans. Roll into 1" balls and place on ungreased cookie sheets. Bake at 350 degrees for 12 to 15 minutes. Let cool a little, then roll in reserved powdered sugar, or sift sugar over them if preferred. Let cool completely. Store layers between waxed paper in containers.

Lace Cookies

Joan Bigg

1 c. oats
2 T. flour
1 t. baking powder
1/4 lb. butter, melted

1/2 c. sugar (less 1 T.)
1 egg
1 t. cinnamon

Combine all dry ingredients. Add liquids to dry ingredients. Mix dough with a wooden spoon. Line cookie sheet with foil and drop 1/2 teaspoon of batter on cookie sheet 3" apart. Bake in 350 degree oven until edges are slightly brown, about 6 to 8 minutes. Let cool completely. Peel off paper and enjoy!

French Pastry Cookies

Renee Smith

1 small pkg. cream cheese
1 stick butter or margarine
1 c. flour

egg white
white or colored sugar

Leave cream cheese and butter out until soft. Knead with flour. Work into a ball and refrigerate overnight. Roll out dough to a 1/8" thickness and cut out with favorite cookie shape. Beat egg white until foamy. Brush cookie top with egg white and dip in sugar. Bake at 350 degrees until golden. Cookie tops will rise and be crispy. You can use colored sugar for a festive holiday cookie.

Cinnamon-n-Sugar Cookie Chips

Di Ann Voegele

10 oz. pkg. flour tortillas
melted butter

cinnamon
sugar

Preheat oven to 325 degrees. Brush melted butter on one side of tortilla. Sprinkle with cinnamon and sugar. Cut tortilla into eighths. Place onto baking sheet that has been lightly sprayed with cooking spray. Bake 10 to 12 minutes or until completely brown. Cool completely. Store in airtight container. Makes about 7 cups of cookie chips.

"When the chips are down, bake cookies."   *Gay Gallagher*

Jim's Favorite Gingersnaps

Wendy Lee Paffenroth

This recipe was created by my son and I when he was about 3. We combined a few recipes until we came up with the right combination!

3/4 c. butter or margarine
1 c. sugar
1/4 c. molasses
4 T. honey
1 large egg

1 t. cinnamon
2 t. baking soda
1 t. ginger
dash of ground cloves
2 to 2 1/2 c. flour

Mix butter, sugar, molasses and honey until well blended. Add egg and mix well again. Add cinnamon, baking soda, ginger and cloves; mix again. Slowly add flour until you can roll the dough into 1" round balls. Roll each ball in granulated sugar and place 2" apart on an ungreased cookie sheet. Bake at 325 degrees until the tops crack and the edges brown up (about 8 to 10 minutes). Makes 3 to 4 dozen depending on size of the cookie.

Maple Nut Cookies

Lisa Embree

My best friend Ann, now 71, walks from her house down the mountain up to my place everyday. She always brings flowers...glorious big blossoms from her garden...and when these are not abundant, she brings cookies. I gave her this recipe and she has added to it our local, delicious, fresh picked elderberries. Sometimes a batch will come with dried cranberries baked in. Ah, the most delicious sort of friendship!

1/2 c. butter
3/4 c. maple syrup
2 c. whole wheat
    pastry flour

1/2 t. salt
1/2 t. baking powder
1 t. vanilla
pecan meats

Preheat oven to 325 degrees. Mix all ingredients together. Roll dough into balls. Flatten out and put a pecan in the middle. Bake about 7 to 10 minutes.

Christmas Cookie Candy Canes

Ronda Stone

My family loves to make cookies for any holiday, but Christmas is our favorite. This cookie recipe is great for that most special holiday.

1 c. milk
4 c. flour
1/4 c. sugar
1 t. salt
1 t. grated lemon peel

1 c. (2 sticks) butter
2 eggs, beaten
1 pkg. dry yeast, dissolved
    in 1/4 c. warm water

Scald milk; let cool to lukewarm. In a large bowl combine flour, sugar, lemon peel and salt. Cut in the butter until like a coarse meal. Add yeast/water, eggs and milk to flour mixture. Combine and stir lightly. Cover and refrigerate for at least 2 hours or up to 2 days. Prepare filling.

Filling:

1 1/2 c. finely chopped apple
3/4 c. chopped nuts (walnuts are best)
1/3 c. sugar
1 1/2 t. cinnamon

Combine all ingredients (a fruit jam can also be used). Divide dough in half and roll out on floured surface to form an 18"x15" rectangle. Spread with 1/2 of the filling. Fold over twice to form three layers (6"x15"). Cut into 15 strips, 6" long. Twist strips and pinch ends to seal. Shape into canes on greased cookie sheet. Bake at 400 degrees for 10 to 15 minutes. Frost to look like candy canes. Using red string licorice, tie around cane cookies and make a bow! Very eye-appealing and all edible. Makes 30 candy canes.

For holiday decorating, I put appropriate cookie cutters in a large clear glass cannister as part of my kitchen's seasonal changes.

Carol Jones

Pumpkin Bar Cookies

Mary Brehm

1/2 c. butter
1 c. sugar
1 c. brown sugar
1 lb. canned pumpkin
2 t. vanilla
4 eggs
1 1/2 c. flour

1 t. baking powder
1/2 t. baking soda
1/4 t. salt
2 1/2 t. pumpkin pie spice
1 c. raisins
1/2 c. chopped nuts
(optional)

Stir butter, sugars, pumpkin, vanilla and eggs over low heat; beat well. Remove from heat and stir in remaining ingredients. Pour into greased jelly roll pan. Bake for 20 to 25 minutes at 350 degrees or until top springs back when touched. Let cool. Top with cream cheese layer.

Cream Cheese Layer:

4 oz. softened
   cream cheese
1 t. vanilla

1/4 t. salt
4 c. powdered sugar
1/3 c. milk

Beat all ingredients together, frost pumpkin layer. Let cool completely. Cut into bars.

You can use your cookie cutters for making french toast! Cut out a variety of designs from raisin bread, dip in batter and cook.
Sift powdered sugar over top and top with syrup.
Serve crisp bacon, fresh fruit and juice alongside.
Also fun to cut out pancakes and folky sandwiches too!

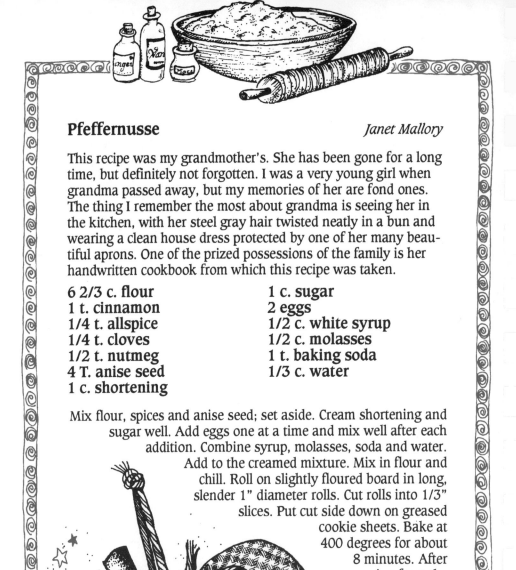

Pfeffernusse

Janet Mallory

This recipe was my grandmother's. She has been gone for a long time, but definitely not forgotten. I was a very young girl when grandma passed away, but my memories of her are fond ones. The thing I remember the most about grandma is seeing her in the kitchen, with her steel gray hair twisted neatly in a bun and wearing a clean house dress protected by one of her many beautiful aprons. One of the prized possessions of the family is her handwritten cookbook from which this recipe was taken.

6 2/3 c. flour
1 t. cinnamon
1/4 t. allspice
1/4 t. cloves
1/2 t. nutmeg
4 T. anise seed
1 c. shortening

1 c. sugar
2 eggs
1/2 c. white syrup
1/2 c. molasses
1 t. baking soda
1/3 c. water

Mix flour, spices and anise seed; set aside. Cream shortening and sugar well. Add eggs one at a time and mix well after each addition. Combine syrup, molasses, soda and water. Add to the creamed mixture. Mix in flour and chill. Roll on slightly floured board in long, slender 1" diameter rolls. Cut rolls into 1/3" slices. Put cut side down on greased cookie sheets. Bake at 400 degrees for about 8 minutes. After removing from the oven, roll immediately in powdered sugar. Store in airtight container. These cookies are best when "aged" for about a week or so before eating.

No-Bake Date Delights

Joan Brochu

15 oz. sweetened condensed milk
1 c. chopped dates (soaked in milk for 10 minutes)
1 c. chopped walnuts (not too small)
2 c. ground graham crackers
2 1/2 c. miniature marshmallows
shredded coconut

In a bowl combine condensed milk and dates. Add walnuts, graham crackers, marshmallows; mix well. Drop by teaspoonsful onto a plate with shredded coconut. Roll well to coat all sides. Stack on waxed paper in the refrigerator to firm and chill. When cold, place in a covered plastic container in your refrigerator. If refrigerated, these will keep up to 3 or 4 weeks.

Orange Balls
Lydia Hall

12 oz. pkg. vanilla wafers
16 oz. pkg. powdered sugar
1/2 c. softened margarine
6 oz. can concentrated frozen
    orange juice, thawed
    and undiluted
1 1/2 c. finely chopped pecans
    or flaked coconut.

Crush wafers to make fine crumbs. Add sugar, margarine and orange juice concentrate, mixing well. Shape dough into 1" balls. Roll balls in pecans or coconut. Chill until firm. Makes approximately 6 dozen balls.

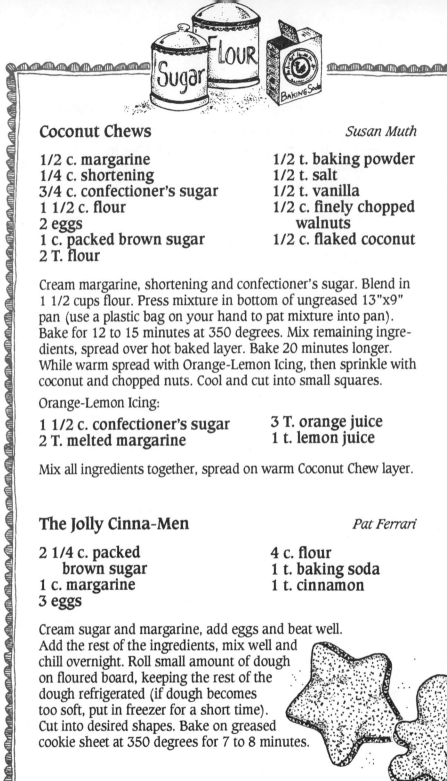

Coconut Chews
Susan Muth

1/2 c. margarine
1/4 c. shortening
3/4 c. confectioner's sugar
1 1/2 c. flour
2 eggs
1 c. packed brown sugar
2 T. flour

1/2 t. baking powder
1/2 t. salt
1/2 t. vanilla
1/2 c. finely chopped
   walnuts
1/2 c. flaked coconut

Cream margarine, shortening and confectioner's sugar. Blend in 1 1/2 cups flour. Press mixture in bottom of ungreased 13"x9" pan (use a plastic bag on your hand to pat mixture into pan). Bake for 12 to 15 minutes at 350 degrees. Mix remaining ingredients, spread over hot baked layer. Bake 20 minutes longer. While warm spread with Orange-Lemon Icing, then sprinkle with coconut and chopped nuts. Cool and cut into small squares.

Orange-Lemon Icing:

1 1/2 c. confectioner's sugar
2 T. melted margarine

3 T. orange juice
1 t. lemon juice

Mix all ingredients together, spread on warm Coconut Chew layer.

The Jolly Cinna-Men
Pat Ferrari

2 1/4 c. packed
   brown sugar
1 c. margarine
3 eggs

4 c. flour
1 t. baking soda
1 t. cinnamon

Cream sugar and margarine, add eggs and beat well. Add the rest of the ingredients, mix well and chill overnight. Roll small amount of dough on floured board, keeping the rest of the dough refrigerated (if dough becomes too soft, put in freezer for a short time). Cut into desired shapes. Bake on greased cookie sheet at 350 degrees for 7 to 8 minutes.

Carmelitas

Portia Walls Palsa

32 vanilla caramels
1/4 c. light cream or evaporated milk
1 roll refrigerator chocolate chip cookie dough
6 oz. pkg. semi-sweet chocolate chips
pecan halves

In top of double boiler, melt caramels in cream, stirring until smooth. Slice cookie dough 1/4" thick and place on bottom of 9"x9"x2" pan, patting to make even crust. Bake at 375 degrees for 25 minutes or until lightly brown. Cool slightly. Sprinkle chocolate chips over warm cookie base. Carefully spread caramel mixture on top. Refrigerate for 1 to 2 hours. Cut into squares and top each piece with a pecan half. Makes 36 pieces.

For the past seven years my mom and I have been having a Christmas cookie exchange. We invite our neighbors and our family to my mom's house, where we first have a nice lunch of hot chicken salad, broccoli cheese soup, homemade rolls, cranberry relish, red and green gelatin (for the season) and apple cider with mulling spices and homemade eggnog. Everyone brings about 5 dozen cookies and after lunch, we exchange. What is nice about it is the togetherness and all the fun we have, not to mention the yummy cookies. Everyone also leaves with a homemade favor that can be placed on their Christmas trees (this year's favors are gingerbread men). We made burlap sacks with apple-cinnamon gingerbread ornaments, a sprig of pine and a little wrapped present. As I said before, our exchange is so fun because we're all together.

Tammy Moon

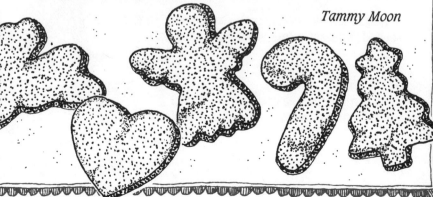

White Sugar Cookies

Sharon Lafountain

My mother used this recipe for holidays and special treats all the while I was growing up. At Christmas time, my brother, sister and I helped with the decorating. As we shared these cookies with friends and family, many asked for the recipe, which we were always happy to share. On one occasion, a teenage friend of mine (we were both 15 at the time) made the cookies for her father, but accidentally switched the amounts of baking powder and baking soda. I still remember the look on her father's face when he took the first bite. It was the first time my mother's cookie recipe did not get rave reviews!

1 t. salt	2 c. sugar
5 t. baking powder	2 eggs
1 t. baking soda	2 t. vanilla
5 c. flour	1/4 t. nutmeg
1 c. shortening	1 c. milk

Combine salt, baking powder, baking soda and flour; set aside. Cream together shortening and sugar. Beat in eggs, vanilla and nutmeg. Add milk alternately with dry ingredients, mixing well after each addition. Chill dough for at least 2 hours. Using approximately 1/4 of the dough at a time, roll out on floured surface and cut with cookie cutters. Bake for 10 to 12 minutes on an ungreased cookie sheet in a 350 degree oven. When cooled, frost with Vanilla Frosting.

Vanilla Frosting:

1/3 c. shortening	3 T. cream or milk
1 T. margarine	1 1/2 t. vanilla
3 c. sifted powdered sugar	

Beat all ingredients together. Can be divided to make several different colors with food coloring.

Love is a homemade cookie...
warm from the oven, served with a smile.

Joy Torkelson

Star Cookies

Constance Cascino

When my children were very small their grandfather had them convinced that at night he hung up the moon, and that their grandmother made the stars. As they grew up, it became a family tradition at Christmas that we all helped to decorate these cookies. Our kitchen table was filled with bowls of different colors of frosting and every cake and cookie decoration on the market, including those hard silver BB's, as we called them. The children had such fun with their beautifully decorated cookies. Somehow they always saved the special "silver" one for me. They were very proud of what they had done. Today, they are grown and have children of their own. This is still my son's favorite cookie, but now his wife makes them and their children help. They all still ask if I'm going to make them. I always do, but their children are now part of the tradition of making "Star Cookies." Needless to say, this recipe has been used by 3 generations of our family already, and I'm sure will be handed down for generations to come.

3 c. all-purpose flour	1 c. butter
1/2 t. baking powder	2 eggs
1/2 t. baking soda	1 c. sugar

Mix flour, baking powder, baking soda and butter like a pie crust. Beat eggs and add sugar. Mix egg/sugar mixture into the flour mixture. Roll dough thin and cut with star-shaped cookie cutter (or any shape you want). Bake on ungreased cookie sheet in 350 degree oven just until edges barely start to brown. Remove onto paper towels to cool. Frost with powdered sugar icing and decorate if desired. Different colors are nice.

Chocolate Jumbles

Barbara Gadfield

This cookie is so chocolatey and moist!

1 c. molasses	4 squares unsweetened
1/2 c. granulated sugar	chocolate
1/2 c. shortening	1 egg
1/4 c. coffee or water	1 t. baking soda
1/2 t. cinnamon	3 c. all-purpose flour
1 t. salt	1/2 t. cloves

Mix sugar, shortening and egg. Melt chocolate and add chocolate and molasses to the sugar mixture. In a separate bowl mix all dry ingredients and spices. Add to the sugar mixture the liquid and then the dry ingredients. Chill dough overnight. Roll dough on floured surface to a 1/4" thickness. Use your favorite cookie cutters to cut out shapes. Bake at 350 degrees for 8 to 10 minutes. Frost with your favorite butter frosting recipe. Decorate with sprinkles and colored sugars.

Cookie Cutter Wrapping Paper

Supplies you will need to make wrapping paper:

brown postal paper
cookie cutters
poster paint

Lay out the paper. Pour poster paint into a flat pan so that you can dip one side of the cookie cutter into the paint. Once you have dipped your cookie cutter, then press it against your paper. Do this many times until your paper is filled with shapes.

Juliana Schneider

Cocoa Dream Cookies

Ferol DeLeon

1/2 c. shortening
2 eggs
1/4 t. vanilla
1 3/4 c. flour
1/2 c. cocoa

1 t. baking soda
1/2 t. salt
1 c. sugar
pecan halves and
    marshmallows

Combine shortening, eggs and vanilla. Sift dry ingredients and add to shortening mixture; mix well. Dough will be stiff. Place pecan halves on a greased cookie sheet. Roll dough into small balls and press one lightly onto each nut. Bake at 350 degrees for 8 minutes. Cut marshmallows in half and place a half-cut side down on each cookie and bake for 3 more minutes (watch carefully not to cook too long). Frost when cool.

Frosting:

1 c. chocolate chips
1/4 c. margarine

1/2 c. milk
1 box powdered sugar

Combine all ingredients except sugar. Cook, stirring until blended. Boil for 2 minutes. Remove from heat and add enough powdered sugar to make easy spreading.

Brown Sugar Almond Bars

Barbara Mann

1/2 c. softened butter
1/2 c. powdered sugar
1 c. flour
3 T. butter
1/2 c. packed brown sugar

1 T. water
3/4 t. lemon juice
3/4 c. sliced almonds
3/4 t. vanilla

Pat softened butter, sugar and flour into an ungreased 9"x9"x2" baking pan. Bake at 350 degrees for 12 to 15 minutes. Melt remaining butter, add brown sugar, water and lemon juice; bring to a boil, stirring constantly. Remove from heat, stir in almonds and vanilla. Spread over crust. Bake 15 to 20 minutes more. Cool. Cut into bars while still warm. Makes 2 dozen.

Peanut Butter Brownies

Katherine Loope

2 c. sugar
1 c. flour
1/2 c. powdered cocoa
1 t. baking powder
1 c. butter or margarine,
    softened

1/2 c. peanut butter
    (smooth or chunky)
4 eggs
1/4 c. milk

Combine sugar, flour, cocoa and baking powder. Add butter and peanut butter; mix well. Add eggs and milk; beat until smooth. Pour into greased 10"x14" pan and bake at 350 degrees for 25 to 30 minutes. Bake until toothpick comes out clean.

☆ ★ ☆

I've always loved the idea of "home baked" Christmas cookies, but most of the efforts I've made turned out terrible. During the past 8 years that I've been married, I found myself too busy to bake from scratch. I found myself very frustrated by all my failures. I finally discovered the solution...ready-to-bake refrigerator dough which can be purchased at the grocery store. I roll chilled sugar cookie dough and cut out Christmas shapes, decorate and bake cookies as directed. For Halloween I even baked "pumpkin" cookies by coloring the sugar cookie dough orange, and cutting with a pumpkin cookie cutter. My favorite "recipe" is peanut butter men, because I really don't like the taste of gingerbread. The peanut butter dough can be rolled and cut with cookie cutters, or you could roll out the dough into a ball (half the size you want the cookies to be) for the head, arms and legs, and one oval for the body. When placing the men on the sheet, don't attach them, leave some space between the head, limbs and body. While baking, they will spread together. The dough needs to be as cold as possible...this helps the cookies keep their shape while baking, and the peanut butter dough gives them just the right color. Now that I have a son (with even less time) I think we'll enjoy making these "homemade" cookies, together, without alot of fuss.

Lori Stricklen

Grandmother's Raspberry Bars

Ildiko Mulligan

My Hungarian grandmother makes a fantastic raspberry bar, but her recipe is quite complicated. Several years ago I came across this simple version that tastes as wonderful as my grandmother's. I recently baked some for a party and several people told me that these raspberry bars taste just like ones their grandmothers make!

2 1/4 c. all-purpose flour
1 c. sugar
1 c. chopped hazelnuts
   (or pecans, or walnuts)

1 c. butter, softened
1 egg
10 oz. jar raspberry
   preserves

Heat oven to 350 degrees. Combine the flour, sugar, hazelnuts, butter and egg in a large mixer bowl. Beat at a low speed, scraping the bowl often, until the mixture is crumbly (about 2 to 3 minutes). Reserve 1 1/2 cups of the crumb mixture. Press the remaining crumb mixture on the bottom of a greased 8" square baking pan. Spread the raspberry preserves to within 1/2" of the edges. Crumble the 1 1/2 cups of reserved crumb mixture over the top. Bake for 45 minutes, or until lightly browned. Cool completely and cut into 2 dozen bars.

Cinnamon Crisps

Linda Detrich

2 pkgs. dry yeast
2 T. sugar
1/2 c. warm water
1/2 lb. margarine
1 T. cinnamon
1 c. sugar

1/2 c. evaporated milk
3 egg yolks
3 c. flour
1/2 t. salt
chopped walnuts

First day: Put yeast, 2 tablespoons sugar and warm water in bowl; let stand for about 5 minutes. Add margarine, milk, yolks, flour and salt; mix well. Put in waxed paper and chill overnight. Second day: Roll about 1/3 of dough into large circle. Sprinkle with chopped nuts and some cinnamon mixture; cut into triangles. Roll from wide end to the tip. Repeat for remaining dough. Place on greased cookie sheet and bake at 325 degrees for 12 minutes.

Cinnamon Mixture:

1 T. cinnamon to 1 c. sugar

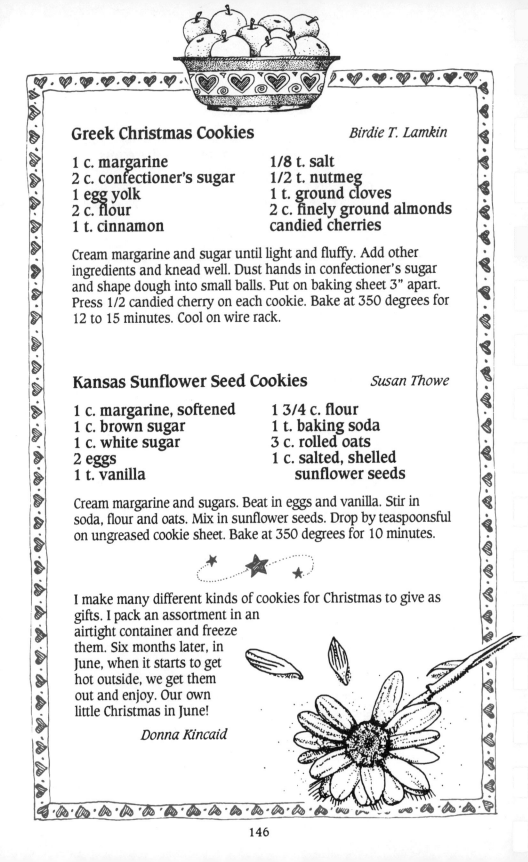

Greek Christmas Cookies

Birdie T. Lamkin

1 c. margarine
2 c. confectioner's sugar
1 egg yolk
2 c. flour
1 t. cinnamon

1/8 t. salt
1/2 t. nutmeg
1 t. ground cloves
2 c. finely ground almonds
candied cherries

Cream margarine and sugar until light and fluffy. Add other ingredients and knead well. Dust hands in confectioner's sugar and shape dough into small balls. Put on baking sheet 3" apart. Press 1/2 candied cherry on each cookie. Bake at 350 degrees for 12 to 15 minutes. Cool on wire rack.

Kansas Sunflower Seed Cookies

Susan Thowe

1 c. margarine, softened
1 c. brown sugar
1 c. white sugar
2 eggs
1 t. vanilla

1 3/4 c. flour
1 t. baking soda
3 c. rolled oats
1 c. salted, shelled
     sunflower seeds

Cream margarine and sugars. Beat in eggs and vanilla. Stir in soda, flour and oats. Mix in sunflower seeds. Drop by teaspoonsful on ungreased cookie sheet. Bake at 350 degrees for 10 minutes.

I make many different kinds of cookies for Christmas to give as gifts. I pack an assortment in an airtight container and freeze them. Six months later, in June, when it starts to get hot outside, we get them out and enjoy. Our own little Christmas in June!

Donna Kincaid

Pippurkakut (Ginger Cookies)

Deirdre Barnett

These fragrant, spicy cookies are good to eat (no icing needed) or for decorating. String with ribbon, jute, or gold cord and use as ornaments, table favors, or package decorations. Hang one on each window pane or set amongst the greenery on the mantle. They bring a spicy scent to the whole house and will last for up to 5 years.

2/3 c. butter, softened	1 1/2 t. ground cloves
3/4 c. packed brown sugar	1 1/2 t. baking soda
1 T. ground cinnamon	2 1/2 c. flour
2 t. ground ginger	1/4 to 1/3 c. water

Cream together butter and sugar. Blend in cinnamon, ginger, cloves and soda. Add flour. Mix in enough water to make a soft, pliable dough. Chill for at least 30 minutes. Preheat oven to 375 degrees. Roll out dough to a 1/8" thickness. Cut with cookie cutters and place cookies on ungreased baking sheet. Make a hole at top of each with a straw, if desired. Bake for 5 to 7 minutes until done. Makes approximately 50, 3" cookies.

Hugs & Kisses Cookies

Cindy Hull

This is a great way to share your hugs and kisses with those you love!

1/2 c. butter
3/4 c. white sugar
3/4 c. brown sugar
1 t. vanilla
2 eggs
1 T. milk
2 1/4 c. flour

1/3 c. cocoa
1 t. baking soda
1 t. salt
1 c. chocolate chips
1 pkg. milk chocolate drops
1 pkg. white chocolate drops

Remove foil wrappers from candies. Beat butter, sugars and vanilla. Add eggs and milk, beat well. Mix in the rest of the dry ingredients. Stir in chocolate chips. Roll into balls and place on ungreased cookie sheet. Bake at 350 degrees for 10 to 11 minutes. Cool for 1 minute. Remove from cookie sheet, press chocolate or white chocolate drop into the center of each cookie.

Cracker Cookies

Sandi Stewart

This fast, quick and super easy cookie recipe is one of my family's favorites. I make these almost every time we're going to the beach to take along. Makes lots and packs great, and I can make them up in a flash.

1 box round buttery crackers
1 lb. almond bark
1 small jar peanut butter
12 oz. pkg. semi-sweet chocolate chips

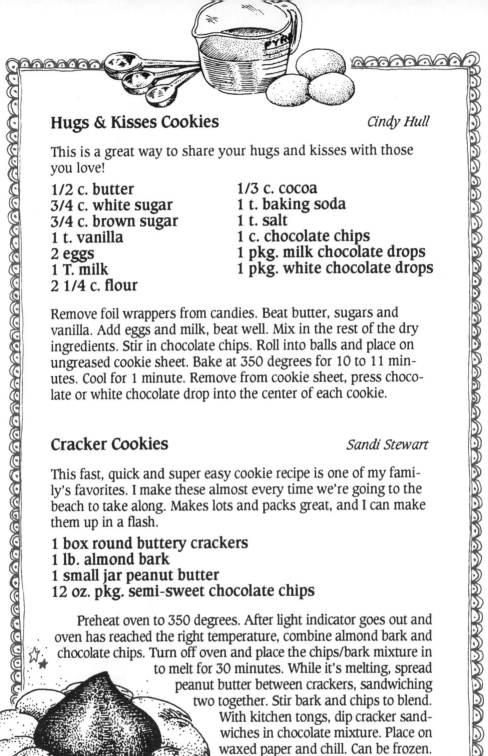

Preheat oven to 350 degrees. After light indicator goes out and oven has reached the right temperature, combine almond bark and chocolate chips. Turn off oven and place the chips/bark mixture in to melt for 30 minutes. While it's melting, spread peanut butter between crackers, sandwiching two together. Stir bark and chips to blend. With kitchen tongs, dip cracker sandwiches in chocolate mixture. Place on waxed paper and chill. Can be frozen.

Pink Clouds

Cindy Ellinger

2 egg yolks
2 1/2 c. flour
1 t. salt
1/2 t. baking powder

3/4 c. sugar
2/3 c. shortening
1/4 c. milk
1 t. vanilla

Mix all ingredients together, blending well. Let chill while preparing meringue. Shape dough into balls using teaspoon. Place on greased cookie sheets, flatten with a glass bottom dipped in sugar. Top each cookie with a teaspoon of meringue. Bake at 325 degrees for 20 to 25 minutes. Makes 42 to 48 cookies.

Meringue:

2 egg whites
1/4 t. salt
1/2 c. sugar
1/2 t. vanilla

1 c. semi-sweet
  chocolate chips
1 c. coarsely chopped
  peppermint

Prepare meringue by beating egg whites in small bowl with salt until soft mounds form. Gradually add sugar, continue beating until soft peaks form. Fold in vanilla, chocolate pieces and peppermint.

For the best results, always use the whites of jumbo eggs to prepare cookies such as meringues and macaroons.

Ernestine Hayes

If some egg yolk should pass into whites while separating, dampen a cloth with cold water, touch yolk and remove.

Deirdre Burton

Holiday Fruit Cookies

Juanita Richardson

These cookies are yummy and best of all, the recipe makes lots. I always add more fruit than what is called for. They freeze well too. This recipe was given to me 25 years ago by an elderly neighbor when I was a young bride.

1 c. soft shortening	1 t. salt
2 c. packed brown sugar	1 1/2 c. pecans, chopped
2 eggs	2 c. candied cherries,
1/2 c. sour milk	halved
3 1/2 c. flour	2 c. dates, chopped
1 t. soda	

Combine shortening, brown sugar and eggs, mixing well. Add sour milk. Sift dry ingredients and stir in. Add pecans, cherries and dates. Let chill. Drop by teaspoonsful 2" apart on greased sheet. Bake at 400 degrees for 8 to 10 minutes. Makes 7 dozen.

Peanut Sitting Pretties

Carla Huchzermeier

For the different holidays I buy the appropriate colored candy-coated chocolate candies...red and green for Christmas; pastels for Easter, etc.

1/2 c. butter or margarine	finely chopped nuts
1/4 c. brown sugar	1 can vanilla frosting,
1 egg, separated	or your own recipe
1/2 t. vanilla	candy-coated milk
1 c. flour	chocolate peanut
1/4 t. salt	candies

Blend butter and sugar in a bowl; stir in egg yolk and vanilla. Sift in flour and salt. Mix well and chill for 1 hour. Roll into 1" balls. Dip into slightly beaten egg white; roll in nuts and bake at 350 degrees for 5 minutes. Press thumb gently in center and bake for an additional 5 minutes. Let cool. Fill thumb print with frosting then top with peanut candy.

★ ☆ ★

Elves' Belly Buttons

Mary Garramone

3/4 c. shortening
1/2 c. sugar
2 eggs
1 t. almond extract
3 oz. box lime gelatin
2 1/2 c. flour

pinch salt
1 t. baking powder
red cinnamon candies
  or maraschino
  cherries, quartered

Cream shortening, sugar and gelatin together. Beat eggs in and add almond extract. Mix dry ingredients together and add gradually to creamed mixture, mixing well. Chill dough overnight. When ready to bake, shape dough into small balls and roll in granulated sugar. Place on greased baking sheet. Make indentation in cookie with thumb and place red cinnamon candy or quartered cherries in depression. Bake at 375 degrees for 10 minutes. Makes approximately 3 to 4 dozen.

Orange Oatmeal Cookies

Joyce Costello

Just dip these cookies in hot tea...taste great!

4 c. flour
2 c. shortening
4 c. sugar
2 T. plus 2 t. baking powder
2 t. salt
2 t. nutmeg
4 eggs

2 T. plus 2 t. grated
  orange rind
1/4 c. orange juice
6 c. rolled oats
  (NOT quick oats)

Heat oven to 375 degrees. Blend flour, sugar, baking powder, salt and nutmeg together. Add shortening, eggs, orange rind and juice; mix well. Stir in oats. Drop by level tablespoonsful on greased baking sheet 2" apart. Bake for 12 to 15 minutes. Can be mixed up in one extra large bowl. This recipe makes a large batch of cookies, but is also easy to halve.

Cherry & Pecan Cookies

Cathy Twohig

1 c. shortening	1 t. baking soda
2 c. brown sugar	1 t. salt
2 eggs	1 1/2 c. pecans
1/2 c. water	2 c. maraschino
3 1/2 c. flour	cherries, cut

Mix all ingredients together. Chill at least one hour. Drop by teaspoonsful on cookie sheet. Bake at 400 degrees for 8 to 10 minutes. Makes 8 dozen.

Chocolate Dipped Creams

Mary Jo Coyne

This recipe is the result of a long standing quest for the perfect, professional-looking cookie to top off a cookie box at Christmas time. This cookie can easily be dressed up with red and green sprinkles on the chocolate glaze before it sets.

1 c. flour, sifted	1 c. butter
1 c. cornstarch	1/2 c. confectioner's sugar

Sift together flour and cornstarch. Cream butter and sugar and work in dry ingredients. Form small balls, about 1/2" in diameter. Place 1" apart on greased cookie sheets. Bake at 375 degrees for 15 to 20 minutes (do not allow to brown). Remove from sheets and roll in confectioner's sugar. Dip cookies in glaze.

Chocolate Glaze:

6 oz. semi-sweet chocolate	2 T. heavy cream
2 T. corn syrup	1 T. butter

Melt all over very low heat or in double boiler.

☆ ★ ☆

I have found that instead of using margarine or butter, a blend of the two works better. Cookies don't flatten out like they do when using only butter or only margarine.

Kathi Stein

Black Walnut & Brickle Chippers

Kathy Horine

3/4 c. shortening
1/2 c. brown sugar
3/4 c. sugar
2 T. milk
1 egg
1 3/4 c. all-purpose flour
1 t. salt
3/4 t. baking soda
1 c. semi-sweet
   chocolate chips

3/4 c. black walnuts
1/3 c. almond brickle chips
1 t. vanilla

Cream shortening, sugars, milk and vanilla; add egg. In a separate bowl combine flour, salt and soda; add to creamed mixture. Stir until combined. Add chocolate chips, black walnuts and brickle. Drop onto ungreased cookie sheets. Bake at 375 degrees for 8 minutes or until golden brown. Makes about 40 cookies. You could also make one large cookie by spooning dough onto a pizza pan and baking at 375 degrees for about 13 minutes. Decorate according to occasion (Happy Birthday, Happy Anniversary, whatever). This dough can be prepared the night before and placed in an airtight container in the refrigerator. Microwave dough on high for 30 seconds to soften a little.

Kisses-n-Hugs Brownie

Susan Muth

1 c. butter
12 oz. pkg. semi-sweet
    chocolate chips
1 1/3 c. sugar
2 t. vanilla
4 large eggs

1 c. flour
1 c. pecans, finely chopped
milk chocolate drops
white chocolate drops
48 foil mini muffin cups,
    paper removed

In a medium saucepan melt butter over low heat. Add chocolate chips, stirring until melted. Remove from heat, stir in sugar and vanilla until blended. Add eggs, one at a time, stirring briskly until blended. Gradually stir in flour until blended; add nuts. Place muffin cups directly onto cookie sheet, then fill cups 2/3 full. Bake at 350 degrees for 20 to 22 minutes (do not overbake), centers should be moist. Remove foil from chocolate drops and place one (milk or white chocolate) on each brownie as soon as removed from oven.

When sending out invitations to a bridal shower, ask each person to bring a family cookie recipe (on a blank card that you include with the invitation). Have a fancy recipe box at the shower to collect these treasures and present them to the bride-to-be. Encourage each person to include the "Romance of the Recipe" (where it originated, whose favorite it is, any remembrances). These memories can be enjoyed for a lifetime.

Wendy Lee Paffenroth

Snicker Doodles

Myra Golubski

This recipe is real old-fashioned and simple, and brings back so many fond memories for me of going to my grandma's house in Ohio. As soon as we walked in the back door we could smell these cookies that she always kept in a tin in the pantry. Sometimes on a blustery winter afternoon, I'll make these cookies, put on a pot of coffee or tea, and just sit for a while and remember grandma.

1/2 c. butter or soft
   shortening
3/4 c. granulated sugar
1 egg
1 1/4 c. flour

1/4 t. salt
1/2 t. baking soda
1 t. cream of tartar
cinnamon and sugar

Cream shortening (or butter) and sugar. Beat in egg. Sift dry ingredients together and add to creamed mixture; stir. Refrigerate for 1 hour. Roll dough into walnut-sized balls and roll in the cinnamon and sugar. Place on ungreased cookie sheet and bake at 400 degrees for 10 minutes. Cool on wire rack. Makes about 24 cookies.

Mini-Cheesecakes

Diane Rupert-Harmon

12 vanilla wafers
2- 8 oz. pkgs. cream cheese
1/2 c. sugar

1 t. vanilla extract
2 eggs
canned chilled pie fillings

Preheat oven to 325 degrees. Line muffin tin with festive colored foil liners. Place one vanilla wafer in each liner. In a bowl mix cream cheese, vanilla extract and sugar on medium speed until well blended. Add eggs and mix well. Pour over wafers, filling 3/4 full. Bake for 25 minutes. Remove from pan when cool and chill in the refrigerator. Top with canned, chilled pie fillings (cherry, blueberry and pineapple are my favorites).

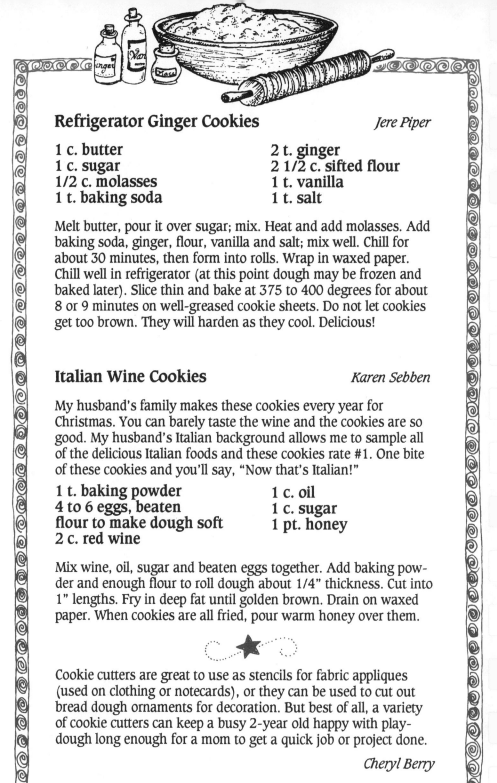

Refrigerator Ginger Cookies

Jere Piper

1 c. butter
1 c. sugar
1/2 c. molasses
1 t. baking soda

2 t. ginger
2 1/2 c. sifted flour
1 t. vanilla
1 t. salt

Melt butter, pour it over sugar; mix. Heat and add molasses. Add baking soda, ginger, flour, vanilla and salt; mix well. Chill for about 30 minutes, then form into rolls. Wrap in waxed paper. Chill well in refrigerator (at this point dough may be frozen and baked later). Slice thin and bake at 375 to 400 degrees for about 8 or 9 minutes on well-greased cookie sheets. Do not let cookies get too brown. They will harden as they cool. Delicious!

Italian Wine Cookies

Karen Sebben

My husband's family makes these cookies every year for Christmas. You can barely taste the wine and the cookies are so good. My husband's Italian background allows me to sample all of the delicious Italian foods and these cookies rate #1. One bite of these cookies and you'll say, "Now that's Italian!"

1 t. baking powder
4 to 6 eggs, beaten
flour to make dough soft
2 c. red wine

1 c. oil
1 c. sugar
1 pt. honey

Mix wine, oil, sugar and beaten eggs together. Add baking powder and enough flour to roll dough about 1/4" thickness. Cut into 1" lengths. Fry in deep fat until golden brown. Drain on waxed paper. When cookies are all fried, pour warm honey over them.

Cookie cutters are great to use as stencils for fabric appliques (used on clothing or notecards), or they can be used to cut out bread dough ornaments for decoration. But best of all, a variety of cookie cutters can keep a busy 2-year old happy with play-dough long enough for a mom to get a quick job or project done.

Cheryl Berry

Nut Cups
(Miniature Pecan Pies)

Kathy-Leigh Russo

With my husband's encouragement, I entered this recipe in our town's country fair...and won a blue ribbon! Along with their being delicious, they are easy to make, can be made in stages, and freeze well.

1/2 c. (1 stick) butter, softened
3 oz. pkg. cream cheese, softened
1 c. flour

Blend together the butter and cream cheese. Add the flour and mix until smooth. By hand, form into 24 balls. Refrigerate for 1 hour or until you are ready to bake the cookies.

Filling:

1 T. butter, melted   **3/4 c. brown sugar**
1 egg   **2/3 c. chopped pecans**
1 t. vanilla

Mix together the butter, egg, vanilla and brown sugar. Stir in chopped pecans. To assemble, place a ball of dough in the cup of a mini-muffin pan. Form the dough into a "crust" inside the cup. Repeat for all 24 dough balls. Spoon 1 teaspoon of filling into each cup (do not overfill). Bake at 325 degrees for 30 minutes or until crust is just golden and filling puffs. Remove from oven and let cool in pans for 10 minutes. Run a sharp knife around the edge of each cookie and remove to a cooling rack. Yield: 24 nut cups.

Glazed Apple Spice Cookies

Marie Skelly

1/2 c. butter or shortening
3/4 c. light brown sugar
1/2 c. molasses
1/4 c. dark brown sugar
1 egg
1/2 t. salt
1 t. cloves
1 t. cinnamon

1/2 t. nutmeg
1 t. baking soda
1 3/4 c. flour
1/4 c. apple juice
1 c. raisins
1 c. chopped walnuts
1 c. diced, unpeeled
   apple (1/4" cubes)

Cream butter, gradually add sugars. Beat in molasses and egg, then add salt, cloves, cinnamon, nutmeg and soda. Add flour and apple juice, mix until smooth. Add raisins, walnuts and apples. Drop level tablespoonsful of batter on greased baking sheet. Bake at 400 degrees for 10 minutes. Remove to wire racks. Spread a little glaze over each cookie while they are still warm.

Glaze:

1 T. butter, softened
1/8 t. salt
1 1/2 c. sifted
   confectioner's sugar

1/8 t. vanilla extract
2 or 3 T. apple juice
1/4 c. finely chopped
   walnuts

In a small bowl cream butter. Add salt, vanilla extract and sugar alternately with apple juice; mix until smooth. Sprinkle with finely chopped walnuts. When cool, store in tightly covered tins.

I seldom use just one kind of nut in my cookies. I chop together pecans, walnuts, peanuts and almonds and use the combination in my recipes. You can freeze the mix and use as needed.

Mary Dungan

Melting Moments

Carol Hanlon

A very rich cookie that goes great with a nice hot cup of tea!

1 c. softened butter	1 c. flour
1/2 c. confectioner's sugar	flaked coconut (optional)
2 T. cornstarch	

In a medium bowl mix together butter, sugar and cornstarch. After well mixed, add flour and mix again; chill dough for a couple of hours. Form balls using 1 tablespoon each. Roll each ball in coconut. Bake at 300 degrees for 25 minutes on ungreased cookie sheet. Another variation, omit coconut, frost and sprinkle with colored sugar. Makes 1 1/2 dozen cookies.

Dog Bones (for people!)

Eileen Hopkins

This is a very simple recipe with a theme my family has a lot of fun with. Dog bone cookie cutters are used and we pipe dog names on every bone, like Rover, Snoopy or Lassie. This has also been a great group activity for Cub Scouts and a favorite family project to celebrate our dog's birthday. My son has also requested them for kindergarten "treat" time. We made one with each child's name on it. These should not be given to animals.

3 oz. unsweetened chocolate	1 egg
2/3 c. butter	1 3/4 c. flour
1/2 t. vanilla	2 t. baking powder
1 1/2 c. sugar	1/4 t. salt
	1/4 t. cinnamon

Melt chocolate and let cool. Cream butter, sugar and vanilla. Stir in egg and cooled chocolate. Add all dry ingredients and mix well. Roll 1/4" thick between waxed paper. Cut with dog bone cookie cutter. Bake for 10 minutes at 350 degrees on ungreased cookie sheet. Let stand for 5 minutes before removing from sheet. Pipe different dog names on bones using store-bought icing.

Swedish Cinnamon Cookies

Gretchen Usawicz

1 c. margarine (or half margarine, half butter)
1 T. molasses
1 T. cinnamon

1 egg yolk
1 1/4 c. sugar
1 t. baking soda
2 1/4 c. flour

Mix all ingredients together well. Form into small balls. Roll in sugar to coat. Place on cookie sheet. Flatten with bottom of glass dipped in additional sugar. Bake at 350 degrees for approximately 10 minutes.

Mint Filled Chocolate Cups

Karen Antonides

1 c. vegetable shortening	3 c. flour
3/4 c. firmly packed	1 t. baking soda
brown sugar	1/2 c. cocoa
3/4 c. sugar	1/2 t. salt
2 eggs, slightly beaten	1 t. vanilla
1/2 c. milk	

Preheat oven to 375 degrees. Grease mini-muffin pan. Cream together sugars and shortening. Add eggs, milk and vanilla; beat well. Add sifted dry ingredients and stir well. Chill dough 15 minutes. With greased hands, take dough and roll into 1" balls. Place a ball in each muffin cup and bake for 10 to 12 minutes. When done, immediately make deep indentation in each cookie with melon baller, forming a cup. Cool for 10 minutes and remove cookies from pan. Cool completely. Makes 4 to 5 dozen.

Filling:

2 cans white frosting	red & green food coloring
mint extract	sugar sprinkles (optional)

Take two small bowls and scrape one can of frosting into each bowl. Add 1 teaspoon of mint extract to each bowl and stir well. Add red food coloring to one bowl, and green food coloring to the other, stirring well. Frosting may be spooned into cookies or may be piped into each cookie using a pastry bag and star tip. Cookies can be topped with sugar sprinkles for an extra festive look. Cookies keep their beautiful shape best if refrigerated.

Crushed candy (peppermint sticks) looks colorful on top of cookies, with either white or pink frosting.

Michele Urdahl

Sandbakels

Cheryl Ott

Here's my recipe for a quick butter-shortbread. It can be made in fancy molds or as sheet cookies or cut out in fancy little hearts. It's great because the ingredients are items we always have on hand. It was given to me by my Grama. She is of Norwegian descent.

1 c. butter
1 c. sugar
2 1/2 c. flour

1 egg
1/2 t. vanilla or
    almond extract

Combine all ingredients. Bake at 350 degrees for 12 to 15 minutes on ungreased cookie sheet. You may add sprinkles to top for a festive look.

Gingerbread Man Advent Chain

You'll need 12 pieces of brown construction paper; fold each in half, with enough room for 2 men on each sheet. Using a cookie cutter or ornament, trace a gingerbread man onto paper, with the head at the fold (you need the heads on both sides of the paper to connect, after you cut them out). Your child can decorate them with glitter, crayons or whatever! On the front, number 1 to 24. On the inside, you could attach a small piece of candy and something written down to do each day (make cookies, sing a song, take a walk to see all the decorations). Then hang them up, all together by string or as a calendar (or even around the tree!).

Michele Moreau

Gingerbread Men

Michelle Dafgek

One of my fondest childhood memories is of our family Christmas tree. Everything on the tree was edible...candy, walnuts, popcorn balls and the best part, gingerbread men. Before baking the gingerbread men, my mother would take a needle and string and thread the string through the cookie. After the cookies baked, we would knot the string and decorate the cookie with icing and it was all ready to hang on the tree. The whole family would decorate the cookies. There would be a cookie decorated for all family members. Couples could be made by baking the cookies with hands touching so that they looked like they were holding hands on the tree. As guests left, my mother would give them cookies to take home, often personalized.

1 c. butter	1 t. ginger
1 c. sugar	2 eggs, well beaten
1/2 c. dark corn syrup	1 t. vinegar
1 t. cinnamon	5 c. flour
1 t. nutmeg	1 t. baking soda
1 t. cloves	

Cream butter with sugar. Add corn syrup and spices. Heat in a saucepan, on stove, stirring constantly. Bring to a boil. Remove from heat and allow to cool. When lukewarm stir in eggs and vinegar. Sift together flour and baking soda. Stir into wet mixture to form a smooth dough. Chill for several hours or overnight. Bake at 350 degrees for 8 to 10 minutes.

For family get togethers (or Christmas office parties), I cut out sugar cookies with a girl and boy cookie cutter and decorate them to resemble family members and friends. I use different colors of icing in the tube and decorator tip to outline the cookies adding hair, clothes, face, eye glasses, etc.

Kim Stevens

Chocolate Peanut Butter Cookies   *Donna Korte*

2/3 c. melted butter   3/4 t. salt
4 c. quick oatmeal   1 t. vanilla
1 c. packed brown sugar   1/2 c. light corn syrup

Mix ingredients well, press into a 10"x15" pan. Bake at 425 degrees for 8 to 10 minutes (don't overbake) until light and golden. They will be bubbly. Cool and frost. Let set before cutting into squares.

Frosting:

12 oz. bag milk chocolate chips
2/3 c. smooth peanut butter

Melt chocolate chips, mix with peanut butter.

Chocolate Peanut Clusters   *Judy Carter*

1/2 lb. sweet chocolate
1 c. peanuts
2/3 c. sweetened condensed milk

Melt chocolate in top of double boiler over boiling water. Remove from heat, add milk and peanuts; mix well. Drop by teaspoonful onto waxed paper.

Make a cookie cutter quilt! Take a cookie cutter and trace around the shape or place chalk around the edges and press on fabric to make the shape. Applique these onto a quilt. These cookie cutter quilts are great for kids of all ages to snuggle under while eating fresh baked cookies.

Pat Meyer

Pistachio Holiday Cookies

Sandy Wisneski

1 c. butter
1 c. sugar
2 eggs, beaten
3 1/4 c. flour
1 t. salt
2 t. baking powder
2 T. milk
1 t. vanilla

1/4 c. nuts, chopped
1/4 c. chocolate-covered
   toffee candy bar pieces
3 3/4 oz. pkg. instant
   pistachio pudding
6 oz. chocolate chips
red food coloring

Cream butter with sugar, add the beaten eggs. Sift flour, baking powder and salt. Add dry ingredients with milk and vanilla. Remove 1/4 dough and add the nuts and candy bar pieces. A few drops of red coloring may be added. Remove 1/4 cup of chocolate chips from bag and set aside. Add the instant pudding and the rest of the chocolate chips to the remaining dough. Shape teaspoons of chocolate chip dough into balls. Flatten and place on greased cookie sheet. Make marble-sized balls from the dough containing the candy bar pieces. Place one on each of the chocolate chip cookie balls and press in one chocolate chip on top. Bake at 375 degrees for 8 to 10 minutes.

Use cookie cutters to make patterns and stitch up simple homespun ornaments... hearts, stars, bells and trees!

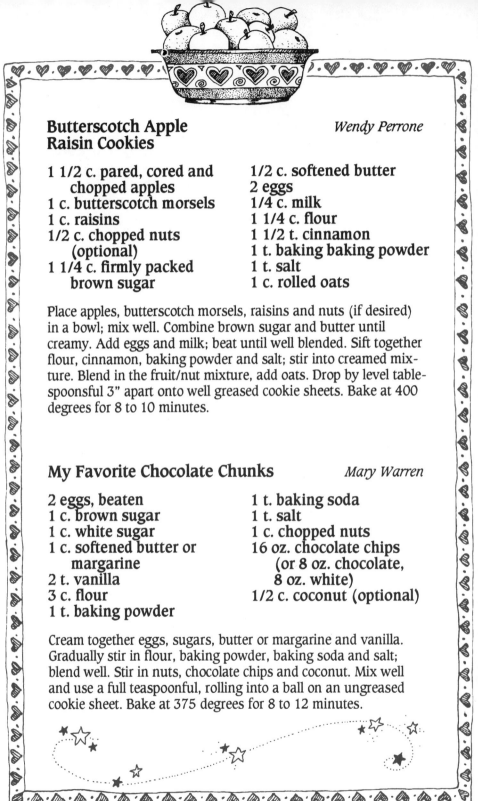

Butterscotch Apple Raisin Cookies

Wendy Perrone

1 1/2 c. pared, cored and chopped apples
1 c. butterscotch morsels
1 c. raisins
1/2 c. chopped nuts (optional)
1 1/4 c. firmly packed brown sugar

1/2 c. softened butter
2 eggs
1/4 c. milk
1 1/4 c. flour
1 1/2 t. cinnamon
1 t. baking baking powder
1 t. salt
1 c. rolled oats

Place apples, butterscotch morsels, raisins and nuts (if desired) in a bowl; mix well. Combine brown sugar and butter until creamy. Add eggs and milk; beat until well blended. Sift together flour, cinnamon, baking powder and salt; stir into creamed mixture. Blend in the fruit/nut mixture, add oats. Drop by level tablespoonful 3" apart onto well greased cookie sheets. Bake at 400 degrees for 8 to 10 minutes.

My Favorite Chocolate Chunks

Mary Warren

2 eggs, beaten
1 c. brown sugar
1 c. white sugar
1 c. softened butter or margarine
2 t. vanilla
3 c. flour
1 t. baking powder

1 t. baking soda
1 t. salt
1 c. chopped nuts
16 oz. chocolate chips (or 8 oz. chocolate, 8 oz. white)
1/2 c. coconut (optional)

Cream together eggs, sugars, butter or margarine and vanilla. Gradually stir in flour, baking powder, baking soda and salt; blend well. Stir in nuts, chocolate chips and coconut. Mix well and use a full teaspoonful, rolling into a ball on an ungreased cookie sheet. Bake at 375 degrees for 8 to 12 minutes.

Christmas Cranberry Roll-Up Cookies   *Charla Viehe*

The red color of these cookies makes them very pretty for the holidays. they are not difficult to make, and it's easy to prepare the dough ahead of time.

2 c. fresh cranberries	1/4 t. salt
1/4 c. sugar	1 1/2 t. cardamon
1 t. orange peel	1/2 c. unsalted butter
1/4 c. finely chopped almonds	3/4 c. sugar
2 c. flour	1 egg
	1 t. vanilla

In a saucepan combine the cranberries, 1/4 cup sugar and orange peel. Add enough water to partially cover. Cook about 15 minutes, or until berries pop and most of water has evaporated. Cool mixture. Combine flour and spices. Cream butter, 3/4 cup sugar, egg and vanilla. Add flour mixture. Divide dough in half. Chill. Roll dough into 12"x7" rectangle on waxed paper. Spread cranberries and almonds over each rectangle. Roll up like a jelly roll, wrap in plastic wrap and chill for at least 2 hours (at this point it can be frozen). Slice roll into 1/4" slices and bake 1" apart on lightly greased cookie sheet at 400 degrees for 12 minutes. Cool completely.

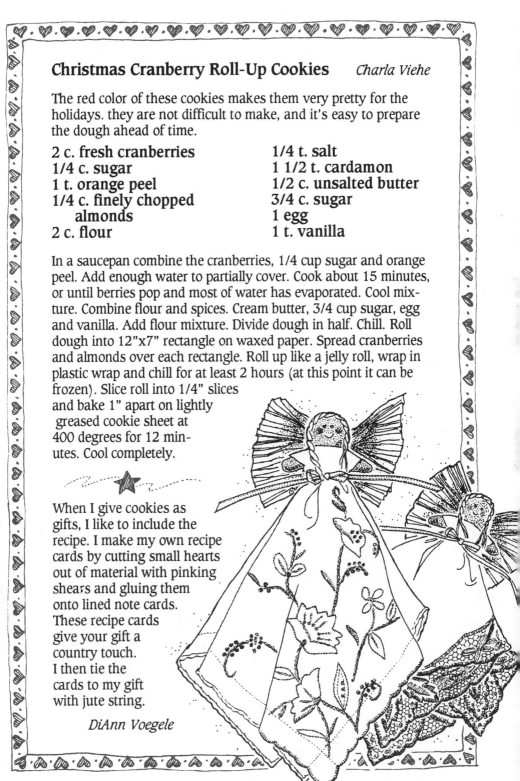

When I give cookies as gifts, I like to include the recipe. I make my own recipe cards by cutting small hearts out of material with pinking shears and gluing them onto lined note cards. These recipe cards give your gift a country touch. I then tie the cards to my gift with jute string.

DiAnn Voegele

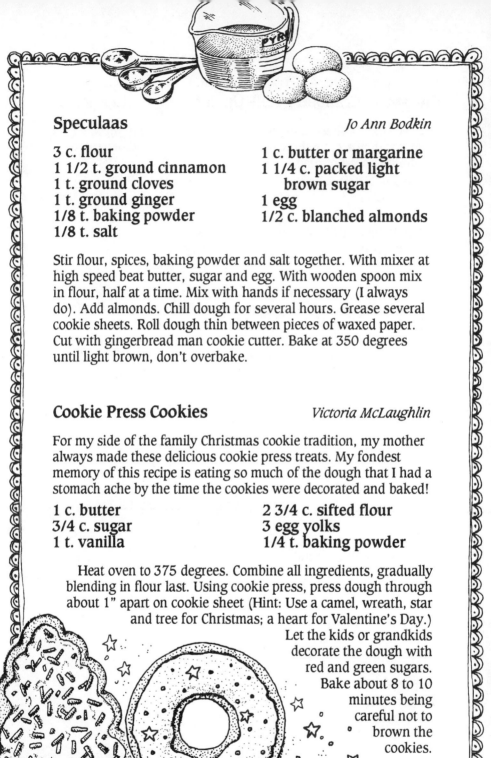

Speculaas

Jo Ann Bodkin

3 c. flour
1 1/2 t. ground cinnamon
1 t. ground cloves
1 t. ground ginger
1/8 t. baking powder
1/8 t. salt

1 c. butter or margarine
1 1/4 c. packed light
  brown sugar
1 egg
1/2 c. blanched almonds

Stir flour, spices, baking powder and salt together. With mixer at high speed beat butter, sugar and egg. With wooden spoon mix in flour, half at a time. Mix with hands if necessary (I always do). Add almonds. Chill dough for several hours. Grease several cookie sheets. Roll dough thin between pieces of waxed paper. Cut with gingerbread man cookie cutter. Bake at 350 degrees until light brown, don't overbake.

Cookie Press Cookies

Victoria McLaughlin

For my side of the family Christmas cookie tradition, my mother always made these delicious cookie press treats. My fondest memory of this recipe is eating so much of the dough that I had a stomach ache by the time the cookies were decorated and baked!

1 c. butter
3/4 c. sugar
1 t. vanilla

2 3/4 c. sifted flour
3 egg yolks
1/4 t. baking powder

Heat oven to 375 degrees. Combine all ingredients, gradually blending in flour last. Using cookie press, press dough through about 1" apart on cookie sheet (Hint: Use a camel, wreath, star and tree for Christmas; a heart for Valentine's Day.) Let the kids or grandkids decorate the dough with red and green sugars. Bake about 8 to 10 minutes being careful not to brown the cookies.

Potato Chip Cookies

Robin Kato

If you don't know what to do with all of those broken potato chips at the bottom of the bag and you want to "wow" your guests every time (plus receive comments about how much weight they're going to gain by this indulgence), make a batch of Potato Chip Cookies to start a new family tradition.

1 lb. butter (or a blend of butter and margarine)
1 c. sugar
2 t. vanilla
1 c. crushed potato chips
3 1/2 c. flour
1 c. mini chocolate chip pieces (optional)

Blend butter, sugar and vanilla; cream well. Add flour, blend. Add crushed potato chips to dough and mix well. An easy way to crush potato chips in a uniform manner is to roll a mayonnaise jar or the like over the bag of chips. If you wish, mini chocolate chip pieces may be added at this time. Drop by teaspoonsful onto ungreased cookie sheet. Bake at 350 degrees for 15 minutes or until edges are slightly golden.

Whenever I go to a sale of any kind, I search for old recipe cards (unused of course). When I give someone special a recipe at holiday time, or whenever, the card may be yellowed with time, but it surely is unique. Since I live solely among antiques in my 100 year old farmhouse, no one is ever surprised. In fact, they are cherished. I cook in a 1916 wood-coal-gas combo stove and love every minute of it.

Deb Damari-Tull

169

Soet Koekies (Spice-Nut Cookies)
Judy Vaccaro

1 c. butter
2 c. brown sugar
4 c. flour
3/4 t. baking soda
2 t. cinnamon
1 t. ginger

1 c. chopped almonds
1 egg
1/4 c. juice (cranberry,
    orange, etc.)
1 beaten egg

In a large bowl, with electric mixer at medium speed, beat butter with sugar until creamy. Mix flour, baking soda, cinnamon and ginger; add almonds. Add flour mixture to butter mixture alternately with egg and juice; blending well. Form into a ball, wrap in waxed paper, then refrigerate until well chilled. Preheat oven to 400 degrees. On a floured board roll out part of dough to 1/4" thickness. Cut out shapes with a cookie cutter. Place on cookie sheet; brush with beaten egg. Bake for 7 to 8 minutes or until golden. Remove to rack to cool. Repeat with the rest of the dough. Makes 6 to 7 dozen.

Nut Sticks
Eileen Commet

1 egg
3 egg yolks
1 c. sugar
4 c. nutmeats, chopped
    very fine

1 t. salt
2 heaping t. corn flakes,
    crushed fine

Beat together egg, egg yolks and sugar. Add nutmeats, salt and corn flakes. Form dough and roll to a 1/4" thickness (this dough will be used as the bottom of your nut stick).

Topping:

3 egg whites   12 T. sugar

Beat egg whites and sugar together. Topping should be firm. Frost dough and cut to form nut sticks (mine are usually 1/2" wide and 1 1/2" long). Place nut sticks on cookie sheet and bake for 1 hour at 200 to 250 degrees (do not overbake).

Toffee Grahams

Diane Dollak

These are quick and easy. A great cookie to make with the little ones who like to arrange the graham crackers and chop and sprinkle the nuts. They are also very tasty.

24 square graham crackers
2 sticks (1 c.) butter
   or margarine

1 c. brown sugar
1 c. chopped walnuts
   or pecans

Preheat oven to 325 to 350 degrees. Arrange cracker squares on a lightly greased cookie sheet with edges around it. In a saucepan bring the butter and sugar to a boil and boil for 2 minutes. Pour over crackers, covering them well. Sprinkle with nuts and bake for about 10 minutes. Cool slightly and cut into 24 squares or 48 "fingers".

★☆★☆★

In Germany, it is the custom on New Year's Eve for the children of the household to place a witch cookie in front of the locomotive on the track of the toy train, which encircles the tree or is located elsewhere in the house. In the morning, the witch cookie lies broken in half on the track and the locomotive is farther down the track having "run over the witch." This portends well for the year to come as once again good triumphs over evil in the destruction of the witch.

Christel Fishburn

171

Rum Balls

Diane Dollak

A very sophisticated addition to a plate of cookies.

1 c. chocolate
   wafer crumbs
1 c. chopped pecans
1 c. powdered sugar

1 1/2 T. white syrup
   or honey
1/4 c. rum or bourbon

Mix all ingredients. Form into small balls and roll in more chopped nuts or powdered sugar. Makes about 6 dozen small balls.

Cookie Cutter Cut-Outs

These cookie cutter cut-outs make great inexpensive little gifts or table favors for both children and adults.

Supplies:

brown paper bags or paper bags
thin polyester fleece
brown thread to match paper
cookie cutters or small patterns (gingerbread boys,
   hearts, etc.)

Cut 2 squares of brown paper the size of cookie cutter plus one inch on all sides. Cut one piece of polyester fleece the same size. Trace cookie cutter in center of one piece of paper. Layer the two pieces of paper, with fleece in between, and stitch on sewing machine on the drawn lines. Cut out with pinking shears slightly outside stitching. Decorate as desired. Add string to hang on the tree. (Example: make eyes and rosy cheeks on gingerbread boys, add a homespun bow tie and glue brown buttons on tummy.)

Corinne McClellan

Jolly Gingerbread Men

Brenda Freese (dedicated to her grandmother, Maurene Moss)

We have a very special closeness in our family that has been passed down for many generations. My grandma always told me that ginger cookies gave a very loving and welcoming aroma to any kitchen and that it was a very special sharing time to bake cookies together.

1 c. butter or margarine (soft)
1 c. sugar
1 egg
1 c. molasses
2 T. vinegar
5 c. all-purpose flour

2 t. ground ginger
1 1/2 t. baking soda
1 t. ground cinnamon
1 t. ground cloves

Beat sugar and butter together until fluffy; add egg, molasses, vinegar and beat well. Next add baking soda, cinnamon, cloves, ginger and flour; beat well until all is well blended. Refrigerate dough 3 hours or until easy to handle. Roll dough 1/8" thick and cut with cookie cutters. Bake in a 350 degree oven for 5-8 minutes, or until done. Cool and decorate as desired.

I made tiny gingerbread boy cookies and hung them with red ribbon on small trees about 2 feet tall. I then gave the trees away as gifts to several people. They loved them and still have them after all these years.

Doodles Young

173

Oatmeal Crispies

Susan Miller

This recipe is very versatile. Add raisins or chocolate chips; bake big or small. At any size, everyone loves this old-fashioned recipe!

1 c. shortening	1 t. salt
1 c. brown sugar	1 t. baking soda
1 c. granulated sugar	1 t. vanilla
2 eggs, beaten	3 c. quick oats
1 1/2 c. flour	1/2 c. walnut meats

Thoroughly cream shortening with sugars; add eggs and vanilla extract; beat well. Add sifted dry ingredients. Add oats and nut meats; mix well. Shape in rolls; wrap in waxed paper and chill thoroughly or overnight. Slice 1/4" thick; bake on ungreased cookie sheet at 350 degrees for 10 minutes. Enjoy!

Brown Butter Refrigerator Cookies

Doodles Young

1 c. butter	1 t. baking soda
2 c. brown sugar	1 t. cream of tartar
2 eggs	1/4 t. salt
3 c. flour	1 c. chopped pecans

Brown the butter, remove from heat and add the sugar; mix well. Add remaining ingredients. Dough will be very stiff. Shape into long rolls and wrap in waxed paper. Chill until firm. These will spread out while baking so place far apart on ungreased cookie sheet. Slice very thin. Bake at 350 degrees for 10 to 12 minutes. Dough will keep for weeks in refrigerator or you may freeze it.

Never, never wash your tin cookie cutters! Thoroughly brush them off when the dough has dried. Then wipe with a clean dish towel.

Pat Akers

Banana Split Bars

Mary Murray

1/3 c. margarine or
   butter, softened
1 c. sugar
1 egg
1 banana, smashed
1/2 t. vanilla
1 1/4 c. all-purpose flour
1 t. baking powder

1/4 t. salt
1/3 c. chopped nuts
2 c. miniature marsh-
   mallows
1 c. semi-sweet chocolate
   chips
1/3 c. maraschino cherries,
   drained and quartered

Heat oven to 350 degrees. Beat margarine and sugar until light and fluffy. Add egg, banana and vanilla; mix well. Mix in flour, baking powder and salt. Stir in nuts. Pour into greased 13"x9" pan. Bake for 20 minutes. Remove from oven and sprinkle with marshmallows, chips and cherries. Bake 10 to 15 minutes longer or until toothpick inserted in center comes out clean. Cool in pan and cut into bars.

Mincemeat Cookies

Charmaine Hahl

1 1/2 c. sifted flour
1 1/2 t. baking soda
1/4 c. water
2 eggs
1/3 c. shortening
3/4 c. brown sugar

1/2 t. cinnamon
1/4 t. nutmeg
1/4 t. salt
1/2 c. nuts
1/2 c. packaged
   mincemeat

Heat oven to 375 degrees. Grease cookie sheets. Sift flour and baking soda together into a large mixing bowl. Put water, eggs, shortening, sugar, spices and salt into blender, cover and process at MIX until smooth. Push CHOP button, remove cover and add nuts and mincemeat, continuing to process only until nuts are chopped. Pour mixture into flour and mix well. Drop by teaspoonful onto cookie sheet. Bake 8 to 10 minutes. Remove from cookie sheet immediately after removing from oven. Yield: about 5 dozen.

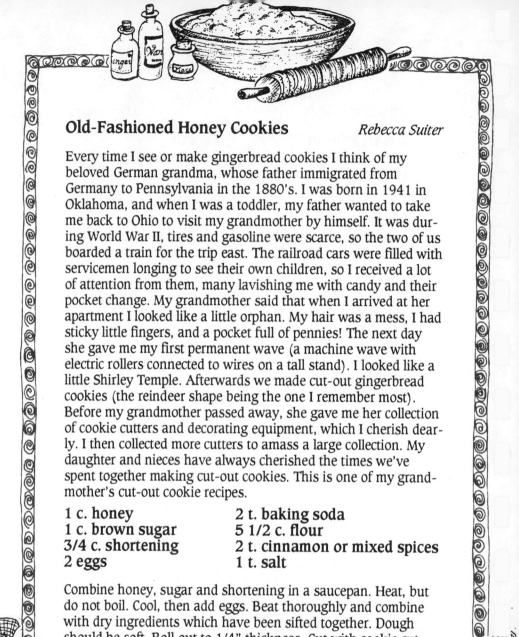

Old-Fashioned Honey Cookies

Rebecca Suiter

Every time I see or make gingerbread cookies I think of my beloved German grandma, whose father immigrated from Germany to Pennsylvania in the 1880's. I was born in 1941 in Oklahoma, and when I was a toddler, my father wanted to take me back to Ohio to visit my grandmother by himself. It was during World War II, tires and gasoline were scarce, so the two of us boarded a train for the trip east. The railroad cars were filled with servicemen longing to see their own children, so I received a lot of attention from them, many lavishing me with candy and their pocket change. My grandmother said that when I arrived at her apartment I looked like a little orphan. My hair was a mess, I had sticky little fingers, and a pocket full of pennies! The next day she gave me my first permanent wave (a machine wave with electric rollers connected to wires on a tall stand). I looked like a little Shirley Temple. Afterwards we made cut-out gingerbread cookies (the reindeer shape being the one I remember most). Before my grandmother passed away, she gave me her collection of cookie cutters and decorating equipment, which I cherish dearly. I then collected more cutters to amass a large collection. My daughter and nieces have always cherished the times we've spent together making cut-out cookies. This is one of my grandmother's cut-out cookie recipes.

1 c. honey	2 t. baking soda
1 c. brown sugar	5 1/2 c. flour
3/4 c. shortening	2 t. cinnamon or mixed spices
2 eggs	1 t. salt

Combine honey, sugar and shortening in a saucepan. Heat, but do not boil. Cool, then add eggs. Beat thoroughly and combine with dry ingredients which have been sifted together. Dough should be soft. Roll out to 1/4" thickness. Cut with cookie cutters. Bake at 375 degrees until golden brown.

Oatmeal-Date Cookies

Gay Hanby

1 c. shortening	1 t. salt
2/3 c. sugar	1 t. baking soda
2/3 c. brown sugar	1 T. cinnamon
2 eggs	1 t. cloves
1 T. vanilla	1 c. oats, uncooked
1 1/2 c. flour	8 oz. pkg. chopped dates

Cream well shortening and sugars. Add eggs and vanilla, beating well. Combine flour, salt, soda, cinnamon and cloves, add to creamed mixture, mixing well. Stir in well the oats and then the dates. Drop by rounded teaspoonsful onto cookie sheets. Bake at 350 degrees for 10 to 12 minutes. Centers will be soft. Cool on wire racks. Makes 5 dozen.

·⋰✩ ★ ✮ ★ ✩·

From the time we were first married, thanks to my Mom's suggestion, we decorated our tree with cookies. I would bake a light colored dough with honey and gingerbread or spice with molasses. I'd cut out holiday shapes, make a little hole at the top with a nutpick (make hole 1/2" from edge), then bake them. After they were cool, I'd frost and decorate them with colored sugar. When the icing hardened, I'd wrap them in plastic wrap and insert a string in the hole to make a loop for hanging...and we had edible tree ornaments! When the children were old enough, they would do the decorating to the sounds of Christmas music on the stereo and they always enjoyed eating "their cookies" when the tree came down. Due to the honey and/or molasses, the cookie was a good keeper and the plastic wrap kept it fresh and clean.

Mrs. William Murphy

Pineapple Drop Cookies

Cindy Peplinski

1/2 c. shortening	2 c. flour
3/4 c. sugar	2 t. baking powder
2 eggs	1/4 t. salt
1 c. crushed pineapple, drained (save juice)	1/4 t. baking soda
	chopped nuts

Mix all ingredients and bake for about 10 minutes at 350 degrees.

Frosting:

6 T. butter	1 t. vanilla
1 1/2 c. powdered sugar	3 T. hot pineapple juice

Mix all ingredients and spread on cookies before they are completely cooled.

Gumdrop Cookies

Jean Stokes

1 c. butter or margarine, softened	1 t. vanilla
	2 1/2 c. all-purpose flour
1/2 c. granulated sugar	1 t. baking powder
1/2 c. packed brown sugar	3/4 c. finely chopped
2 T. milk	gumdrops

Cream together butter and sugars, beat in milk and vanilla. Stir together flour and baking powder, blend into creamed mixture. Stir in gumdrops. Shape dough into two 14" rolls. Wrap in waxed paper or clear plastic wrap. Chill thoroughly. Cut into 1/4" slices. Place on ungreased cookie sheet. Bake at 375 degrees for about 10 minutes. Makes about 9 dozen.

I'm an RN and for our Christmas party I made a batch of "nurse" cookies. Everyone had fun picking themselves out of the batch!

Kim Stevens

Mocha Truffle Cookies

Bernice Ladroot

1/2 c. margarine or butter
1/2 c. semi-sweet
   chocolate pieces
   plus 1 c.
1 T. instant coffee crystals
3/4 c. sugar
3/4 c. packed brown sugar

2 eggs
2 t. vanilla
2 c. flour
1/3 c. unsweetened
   cocoa powder
1/2 t. baking powder
1/4 t. salt

In a large saucepan melt margarine or butter and the 1/2 cup chocolate pieces over low heat. Remove from heat. Stir in coffee crystals. Cool for 5 minutes. Stir in sugars, eggs and vanilla. In a medium mixing bowl combine flour, cocoa, baking powder and salt. Stir into coffee mixture. Stir in the 1 cup chocolate pieces. Drop by tablespoonsful on greased sheets. Bake at 350 degrees for 10 minutes.

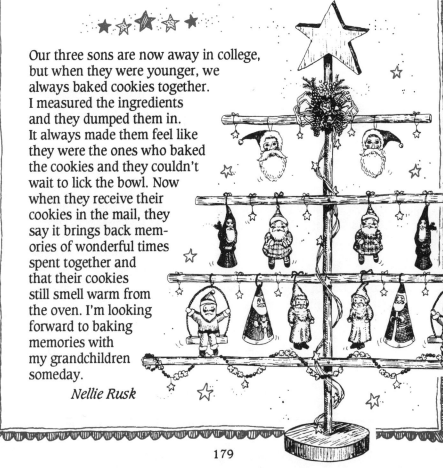

Our three sons are now away in college, but when they were younger, we always baked cookies together. I measured the ingredients and they dumped them in. It always made them feel like they were the ones who baked the cookies and they couldn't wait to lick the bowl. Now when they receive their cookies in the mail, they say it brings back memories of wonderful times spent together and that their cookies still smell warm from the oven. I'm looking forward to baking memories with my grandchildren someday.

Nellie Rusk

Zucchini Bar Cookies

Cathy Weaver

3/4 c. margarine, softened	1 3/4 c. flour
1/2 c. sugar	1 1/2 t. baking powder
1/2 c. brown sugar	2 c. shredded zucchini
1 t. vanilla	1 c. coconut
2 eggs	3/4 c. walnuts

Combine margarine, sugars and vanilla; beat until fluffy. Beat in eggs, one at a time. Add flour, baking powder, zucchini, coconut and walnuts. Spread in greased jelly roll pan. Bake at 350 degrees for 40 minutes. Frost with glaze while still warm.

Glaze:

1 c. powdered sugar	1 T. melted margarine
1 t. vanilla	1 t. cinnamon
2 T. milk	

Combine ingredients, glaze zucchini bars.

Pecan White Chip Cookies

Pat Akers

1 1/4 c. all-purpose flour	1 t. vanilla extract
1/2 t. baking soda	2/3 c. coarsely chopped
1/2 c. butter	pecans
3/4 c. packed brown sugar	2/3 c. white chocolate
1 large egg	chips

Heat oven to 350 degrees. Mix flour and baking soda. Cream butter, sugar, egg and vanilla. With mixer at low speed, gradually add flour mixture. Beat just until blended. Stir in pecans and chips. Drop by rounded teaspoonful on ungreased cookie sheets. Bake 11 to 13 minutes until edges are lightly browned. Tops will feel soft. Cool on cookie sheets for 2 to 3 minutes before removing to racks to finish cooling. Ummm good!

PANTRY

Grandma's Old-Fashioned Sugar Cookies

Dyan Janov-Nugent

This delicious recipe has been handed down for four generations, originating with my grandmother. Since baking these cookies was an activity we enjoyed together, fond memories of her come to mind every time I bake a batch.

1/2 c. oil	1 t. vanilla
1/2 c. margarine	2 1/2 c. flour
1/2 c. sugar	1/2 t. salt
1/2 c. powdered sugar	1 t. baking soda
1 egg	1/2 t. cream of tartar

Cream oil, margarine, sugars, egg and vanilla. In a separate bowl, mix flour, salt, baking soda and cream of tartar. Gradually add to sugar mixture and blend well. Chill dough until firm. Form into 1" balls and place on cookie sheet. Press cookies with the bottom of a glass or a cookie press dipped in sugar. Bake at 350 degrees for 8 to 10 minutes.

Peanut Butter Spotlights

Lin Ferrol

1 box yellow cake mix	2 eggs
1/2 c. peanut butter	1 c. candy coated peanut
1/4 c. margarine or butter	butter pieces
1/4 c. water	

Mix together all ingredients except candy pieces. Fold in candy. Drop by rounded teaspoonful onto ungreased cookie sheet, 2" apart. Bake at 350 degrees for 8 to 12 minutes. Each cookie has 100 calories. Makes 3 1/2 dozen cookies.

When piping icing on cookies, if you don't have decorator bags or tips, just take a sandwich bag and cut off the tip of a corner. Fill the bag with icing, lightly squeeze bag and decorate.

Michele Urdahl

Thumbprint Pies

Lisa Prichard

1 1/4 c. flour
3 T. sugar

1/2 c. butter (must be butter)
preserves

Stir together flour and sugar. Cut in butter until fine crumbs. Form mix into a ball, and knead until smooth. Shape into 1" balls. Place on ungreased cookie sheet. Make thumbprint in center of ball, reshape if necessary. Bake at 325 degrees for 18 minutes until bottoms and edges are light brown. Remove from oven and immediately spoon favorite preserves into each thumbprint. Cool completely and then remove from sheet.

Aunt Hilda's Blondies

Anne Farnese

My contribution to our annual family gathering is a big batch of butterscotch brownies which my family calls "blondies". I bake them to remember my Aunt Hilda whose baked goods were legendary in our family. She gave me the recipe a few years before she died and it is one of my cherished possessions.

1/2 c. butter
1 1/2 c. light brown sugar
2 eggs

1 1/2 t. pure vanilla extract
1 1/2 c. flour
2 t. baking powder

Preheat oven to 350 degrees. Melt butter in large saucepan. Remove from heat. Blend in sugar. Add eggs, beat well one at a time. Add vanilla extract. Add baking powder and flour. Pour into greased 13"x9"x2" pan. Bake for 25 to 30 minutes. When completely cooled, cut into approximately 1 1/2" squares.

When you visit a discount china store and they advertise plates or platters fairly inexpensively, purchase several to use for special homemade gifts of food. Wrap them in pretty cellophane, tie with fabric ribbon and bows and give to friends and neighbors during the holidays. Large platters with an array of cookies or bread slices, with fresh greens and berries, is a beautiful and most thoughtful gift of friendship.

Jan Kouzes

Glazed Fresh Apple Cookies

Jennifer Muller

1/2 c. butter
1 egg
1/2 t. baking soda
1/2 t. salt
1 c. chopped nuts
1 c. unpeeled apple, finely
   chopped

1 1/3 c. brown sugar
2 c. flour
1/2 t. nutmeg
1 t. baking powder
1 t. cinnamon
1/4 c. apple juice or milk
1 c. raisins

Preheat oven to 400 degrees. Thoroughly cream butter and sugar. Add egg and beat well. Sift together flour, baking soda, baking powder, salt, cinnamon and nutmeg. Add to creamed mixture alternately with apple juice. Stir in nuts, raisins and apples. Drop by tablespoonsful on greased cookie sheets. Bake for 10 to 12 minutes. Remove cookies from pan at once and glaze while cookies are still hot. Makes 4 dozen.

Glaze:

1 T. butter
1 1/2 c. confectioner's sugar
1/8 t. salt
1/4 t. vanilla

2 1/2 T. apple juice
  or milk

Mix butter, sugar and salt. Stir in apple juice and vanilla.

When rolling out chocolate cookie dough, sprinkle rolling surface with cocoa instead of flour. There will be no unsightly white flour to mar surface of chocolate cookies and cookies will have an even more intense chocolate flavor.

Tamara Gruber

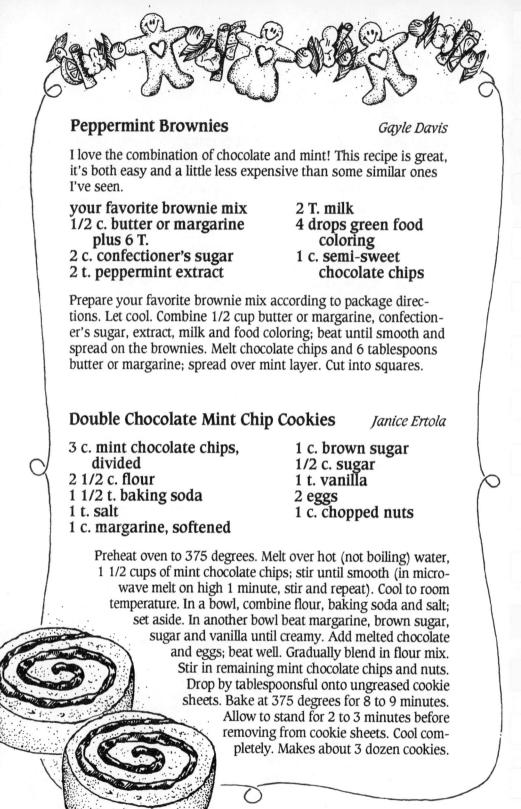

Peppermint Brownies
Gayle Davis

I love the combination of chocolate and mint! This recipe is great, it's both easy and a little less expensive than some similar ones I've seen.

your favorite brownie mix
1/2 c. butter or margarine plus 6 T.
2 c. confectioner's sugar
2 t. peppermint extract

2 T. milk
4 drops green food coloring
1 c. semi-sweet chocolate chips

Prepare your favorite brownie mix according to package directions. Let cool. Combine 1/2 cup butter or margarine, confectioner's sugar, extract, milk and food coloring; beat until smooth and spread on the brownies. Melt chocolate chips and 6 tablespoons butter or margarine; spread over mint layer. Cut into squares.

Double Chocolate Mint Chip Cookies
Janice Ertola

3 c. mint chocolate chips, divided
2 1/2 c. flour
1 1/2 t. baking soda
1 t. salt
1 c. margarine, softened

1 c. brown sugar
1/2 c. sugar
1 t. vanilla
2 eggs
1 c. chopped nuts

Preheat oven to 375 degrees. Melt over hot (not boiling) water, 1 1/2 cups of mint chocolate chips; stir until smooth (in microwave melt on high 1 minute, stir and repeat). Cool to room temperature. In a bowl, combine flour, baking soda and salt; set aside. In another bowl beat margarine, brown sugar, sugar and vanilla until creamy. Add melted chocolate and eggs; beat well. Gradually blend in flour mix. Stir in remaining mint chocolate chips and nuts. Drop by tablespoonsful onto ungreased cookie sheets. Bake at 375 degrees for 8 to 9 minutes. Allow to stand for 2 to 3 minutes before removing from cookie sheets. Cool completely. Makes about 3 dozen cookies.

Peppermint Pinwheels

Jennifer Bolton

4 c. flour
1 t. baking powder
1 t. salt
1 1/4 c. (2 1/2 sticks)
   butter or margarine,
   softened

1 1/2 c. sugar
2 eggs
1 t. vanilla
1 t. peppermint extract
red and green
   food coloring

Beat butter with sugars until fluffy with electric beater at high speed. Beat in eggs, vanilla and peppermint. Stir in dry ingredients to make a soft dough. Tint small amount of dough green and roll into long rope. Divide rest of dough in half. Tint half with red food coloring. Roll out one plain piece of dough to a 14"x3" rectangle between sheets of waxed paper. Repeat with red dough. Chill doughs and rope in freezer for 10 minutes or until firm. Place red dough (pulling off paper) on plain dough. Place green rope on long edge then roll up into pinwheel. Refrigerate 4 hours. Slice 1/4" thick. Place on greased cookie sheets. Bake at 350 degrees for 10 minutes. Cool on wire racks. Makes about 6 dozen.

Did you know the term "brownie" wasn't always applied to the fudgy bar we know today? Some 19th century brownies were made with chopped nuts, but no chocolate. Others were drop cookies and some bar cookies resembling modern-day brownies were called "Indians".

Mary Murray

A poem, **The Cookie Jar**
by Elsie Duncan Yale starts with:

You may talk about your vases,
Just how beautiful they are.
But to me there's nothing nicer,
Than a well-filled cookie jar.

Gay Gallagher

English Toffee Cookies

Jennifer Bolton

1 c. sugar
1 c. butter
1 egg yolk

1 t. vanilla
1 c. ground pecans
2 c. flour

Cream butter and sugar. Add egg yolk, 1/2 cup ground pecans, flour and vanilla. Press into greased 13"x9" pan. Spread with unbeaten egg white on top and remaining pecans. Bake in slow (300 degree) oven for 45 minutes or until light brown. Cut at once.

Crunchy Chip Cookies

Debi Pflug

1 c. butter or margarine
1/2 c. sugar
1 1/2 c. packed brown sugar
2 eggs
1 1/2 t. vanilla
2 c. all-purpose flour

1 t. baking soda
1/2 t. salt
2 c. quick cooking oats
12 oz. pkg. semi-sweet
    chocolate pieces
2 c. chow mein noodles

Beat butter and sugars until creamy and fluffy; beat in eggs and vanilla. Gradually add dry ingredients, mix well. Stir in oats, chocolate pieces and noodles. Drop by teaspoonsful on greased cookie sheet 2" apart. Bake at 350 degrees for 10 to 12 minutes. Remove to wire rack to cool. Makes 7 dozen.

Over the years, I started collecting cookie cutters. Even before our children were born, my mother-in-law who was charmed by my efforts, bought an antique cookie cutter for my collection. As time went on, I began to buy two of each cutter so that each of my daughters would have her own collection. In addition, I have developed my own recipe book by putting all our family favorites on the computer and keeping an up-to-date set of recipes. When my daughters leave home, they will each have a collection of cutters and recipes all of which are filled with many fond memories.

Nell McDaniel

Angel Wing Cookies

Kara Bacon

I first encountered these delightful cookies when I visited my aunt who was living in the Netherlands. I immediately assumed she had discovered some wonderful European recipe because these cookies are so fine, delicate and heavenly...just like angels' wings. Was I surprised to discover that the recipe actually came from a church cookbook from her hometown in Iowa!

1 c. brown sugar	1 t. baking soda
1 c. white sugar	1 t. cream of tartar
1 c. butter	3 c. flour
1 c. oil	1 1/2 c. quick cooking
1 egg, beaten	oatmeal
1 t. salt	2 c. crispy rice cereal

Cream together the brown sugar, white sugar and butter. Add oil and egg and beat until creamy. Sift together salt, baking soda, cream of tartar and flour; add to creamed mixture. Blend in oatmeal and cereal. Chill overnight. Drop by tablespoon onto ungreased baking sheets. Bake for 10 to 12 minutes at 350 degrees. Because these cookies are so delicate, they require special care, so be careful when storing them.

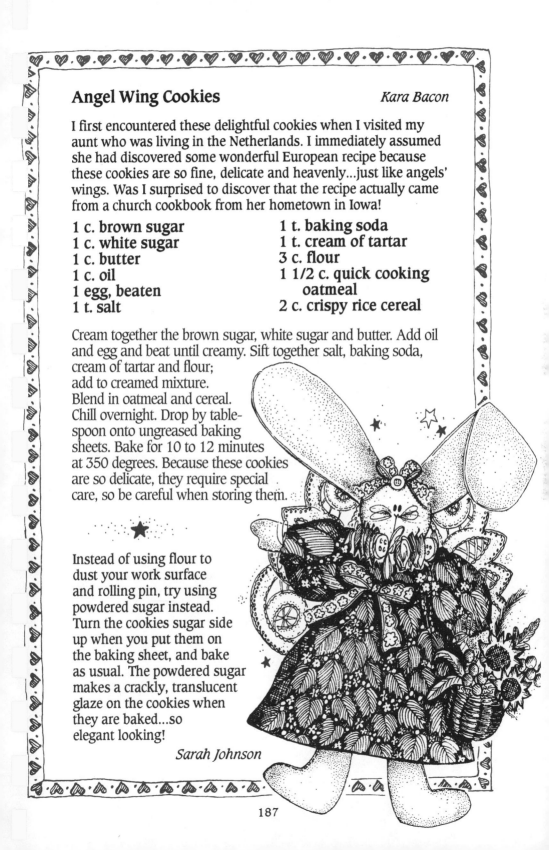

Instead of using flour to dust your work surface and rolling pin, try using powdered sugar instead. Turn the cookies sugar side up when you put them on the baking sheet, and bake as usual. The powdered sugar makes a crackly, translucent glaze on the cookies when they are baked...so elegant looking!

Sarah Johnson

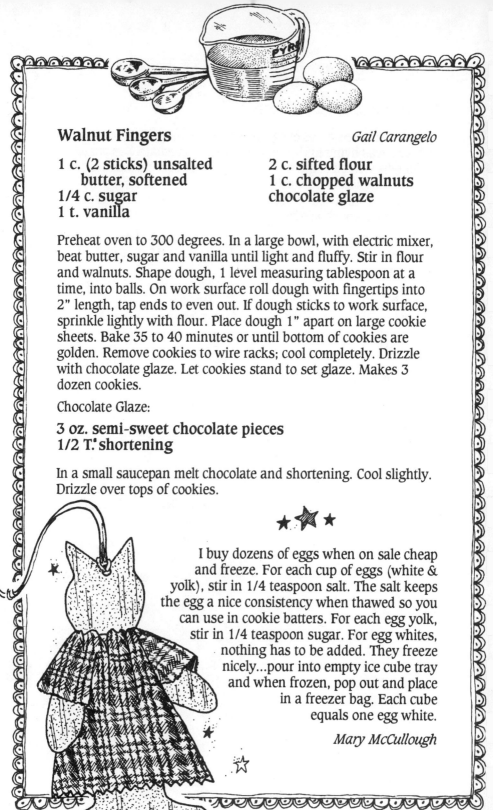

Walnut Fingers

Gail Carangelo

1 c. (2 sticks) unsalted
    butter, softened
1/4 c. sugar
1 t. vanilla

2 c. sifted flour
1 c. chopped walnuts
chocolate glaze

Preheat oven to 300 degrees. In a large bowl, with electric mixer, beat butter, sugar and vanilla until light and fluffy. Stir in flour and walnuts. Shape dough, 1 level measuring tablespoon at a time, into balls. On work surface roll dough with fingertips into 2" length, tap ends to even out. If dough sticks to work surface, sprinkle lightly with flour. Place dough 1" apart on large cookie sheets. Bake 35 to 40 minutes or until bottom of cookies are golden. Remove cookies to wire racks; cool completely. Drizzle with chocolate glaze. Let cookies stand to set glaze. Makes 3 dozen cookies.

Chocolate Glaze:

3 oz. semi-sweet chocolate pieces
1/2 T. shortening

In a small saucepan melt chocolate and shortening. Cool slightly. Drizzle over tops of cookies.

★ ✦ ★

I buy dozens of eggs when on sale cheap and freeze. For each cup of eggs (white & yolk), stir in 1/4 teaspoon salt. The salt keeps the egg a nice consistency when thawed so you can use in cookie batters. For each egg yolk, stir in 1/4 teaspoon sugar. For egg whites, nothing has to be added. They freeze nicely...pour into empty ice cube tray and when frozen, pop out and place in a freezer bag. Each cube equals one egg white.

Mary McCullough

Pastel Coconut Bon Bons

Marge Reeland

3 oz. pkg. cream cheese
2 1/2 c. powdered sugar
1/4 t. vanilla

dash of salt
green food coloring
1/3 to 1/2 c. flaked coconut

Mix and refrigerate for 1 hour. Shape into balls and roll in coconut. Refrigerate until firm.

Snowballs

Bernadine Sabia

1 c. butter or margarine, softened
1/3 c. plus 1 T. confectioner's sugar

2 t. vanilla extract
2 c. flour
2 c. chopped walnuts

Cream butter and sugar with an electric mixer. Add separately the vanilla, flour and then nuts, mixing after each addition. Chill dough for 1 hour. Shape rounded teaspoonsful of dough into balls. Bake on ungreased cookie sheets at 350 degrees for approximately 18 minutes. Do not brown. Roll hot baked cookies in confectioner's sugar. Makes approximately 60 cookies.

When we were selling our house, I kept balls of cookie dough (frozen on cookie sheets, then transferred to tins) on hand. Then I would put 6 balls on a small pan in the toaster oven just before a showing. Before we scooted out the door, just ahead of the prospective buyer's arrival, I had hot cookies on a plate with a note, "Please help yourself!"

Candy Hannigan

Ginger Pennies

Karla Nitz

These are not Pfeffernusse. Ginger Pennies are crisp little coin-sized cookies which look like those cookie dough droplets that accidentally get baked when making cookies. It's a German recipe handed down and is especially loved by coffee drinkers who enjoy a few Ginger Pennies in the early morning. Each batch makes several hundred (I've never actually counted the number it makes...perhaps 1,000's!)

1 1/2 c. flour
3/4 t. ginger
3/4 t. cinnamon
1/2 t. baking soda
1/4 t. salt
1/2 t. ground cloves

1 c. firmly packed
   brown sugar
1 large egg
1/4 c. unrefined molasses
12 T. unsalted butter,
   softened

Sift together flour, ginger, cinnamon, baking soda, salt and cloves. Cream together brown sugar, egg, molasses (grease the measuring cup before pouring molasses into it) and butter. Beat dry mixture into wet mixture and mix together. Scrape mixture into a gallon size zippered plastic food bag. Cut off small lower corner of bag and pipe small dots (about 1/8 teaspoon or a 1 1/2" mound) about 1" apart on greased baking sheet. Bake in preheated 325 degree oven for 3 (three) minutes and then slide off. Let cool and crisp. These keep for several months in airtight container at low humidity.

★ ☆ ★ ☆ ★

Molasses will slip out of a measuring cup easily if you lightly oil the cup before adding the molasses.

Ernestine Hayes

That's the way the cookie crumbles.
— Saying (1950's)

Lemon Snap Cookies

Heather Hood

These are wonderfully light and so simple. I've also tried other flavored cake mixes, such as chocolate, but lemon is still my favorite.

1 pkg. (2 layer size) lemon cake mix
4 1/2 oz. carton frozen whipped topping, thawed
1 egg, beaten
powdered sugar

Blend cake mix, whipped topping and egg together. Shape rounded teaspoonsful of dough into balls. Roll in powdered sugar. Place on greased cookie sheets. Bake at 350 degrees for about 12 minutes or until golden. Makes about six dozen.

Buckwampun Farm Breakfast Cookies

Helene Hamilton

A great, nutritious cookie for breakfast on the run!

1 c. sugar
1/2 c. butter
1 egg
1 t. vanilla
1 c. all-purpose flour

1/2 t. baking soda
1/4 t. salt
2 c. raisin bran cereal
1/2 c. plus raisins

Preheat oven to 350 degrees. Beat sugar and butter until fluffy. Add egg and vanilla to sugar mixture. Sift flour, baking soda and salt together and stir into creamed mixture. Add raisin bran and raisins, mixing well. Drop by teaspoonsful onto lightly greased cookie sheets. Bake for about 11 to 13 minutes for chewy cookies (best) or about 15 minutes for crispy cookies.

★ ☆ ✬ ☆ ★

When decorating cinnamon cookie ornaments, use squeeze-on fabric paints for accents, just as you would use frosting.

Donna Olmstead

Sugar Cookies

Debra Felt

We enjoy a wonderful generational cookie tradition. As each holiday (Valentine's, Easter, Thanksgiving, Christmas and others) approaches, my mother, affectionately known as "Grammie", invites my daughters to her home for a "Cookie-Dough Day." On Cookie-Dough Day, they make, roll and cut out sugar cookies. After baking, the frosting and decorating begins. Not only do my daughters enjoy the baking, decorating and eating of the cookies, but also hearing stories of my mother's childhood memories and her reminiscences of her mother. Thus the memories are passed to another generation. Life seems much more bearable when there is a Cookie-Dough Day to look forward to.

1 1/2 c. sifted confectioner's sugar	1/2 t. almond flavoring
	2 1/2 c. flour
1 c. butter	1 t. baking soda
1 egg	1 t. cream of tartar
1 t. vanilla	

Cream butter and sugar. Mix in egg and flavorings. Blend dry ingredients and stir in. Refrigerate 2 to 3 hours. Divide dough in half. Roll out on lightly floured pastry cloth. Cut out desired shapes. Bake at 375 degrees for 7 to 8 minutes.

Scotch Teas

Diane Dollak

A wheat free cookie that's easy to make!

1 c. butter	2 t. baking powder
2 c. brown sugar	1/2 t. salt
	4 c. quick oats (not instant)

In a saucepan, melt the butter and brown sugar. Add remaining ingredients. Pour into a 13"x9"x2" pan and bake at 350 degrees for 20 to 25 minutes. Cut into small squares or bars. Makes about 4 dozen.

Valentine Cookies

Kathy Grashoff

These cookies are fun to decorate and to write your own special messages on!

1/2 c. butter
3/4 c. packed brown sugar
1 t. vanilla
1 egg
1 c. plus 2 T. flour

1/2 t. baking soda
1/2 t. salt
6 oz. pkg. chocolate chips
1/2 c. chopped walnuts

Grease two heart-shaped pans. In a large bowl beat the butter and brown sugar until creamy. Beat in the vanilla and the egg. Mix in the flour, soda and salt. Then add the chocolate chips and nuts. Divide dough in half and spread in pans. Bake for 10 to 15 minutes at 375 degrees. Cool in the pans for 10 minutes, then remove and cool completely. Yield: Two big cookies.

Cranberry Nut Swirls

Sandra Bowman

These are especially nice for Christmas. They look so pretty on a tray with iced cookies and are so delicious!

1/2 c. softened butter
3/4 c. sugar
1 egg
1 t. vanilla
1 1/2 c. all-purpose flour
1/4 t. baking powder
1/4 t. salt

1/2 c. finely ground cranberries
1/2 c. finely chopped walnuts
1 T. grated orange peel
3 T. brown sugar
2 t. milk

Combine the butter, sugar, egg and vanilla, beat until light and fluffy. Combine the dry ingredients and add to creamed mixture. Refrigerate for at least 1 hour. In a small bowl combine walnuts, cranberries and orange peel. On a floured surface roll the dough into a 10" square. Combine brown sugar and milk and spread over dough. Sprinkle with the cranberry mixture and roll up tightly. Wrap with waxed paper and chill for several hours. Cut into 1/4" slices. Bake on a well greased cookie sheet at 375 degrees for 14 minutes.

Portuguese Suspiros (Sighs)

Diane Dollak

These are elegant, no fat, no wheat cookies. Keep them dry in a tight tin.

3 egg whites
1/4 t. cream of tartar
1/2 c. sugar

1/4 c. chopped almonds
1 t. grated lemon peel

Beat egg whites with cream of tartar until foamy. Gradually add sugar and beat until stiff. Fold in almonds and lemon peel and drop by teaspoonsful onto cookie sheets. Bake at 325 degrees for 25 minutes, until light tan. Makes 2 to 3 dozen.

Party Cookies

Sandy Bessingpas

You can vary the candy coated milk chocolate pieces to correspond to the season. Red and green for Christmas, pastels for Easter, orange and brown for Halloween. Everyone loves them!

1 c. margarine
1 c. packed brown sugar
1/2 c. white sugar
2 t. vanilla
2 eggs

2 1/4 c. flour
1 t. baking soda
1 c. candy coated milk
  chocolate pieces

Cream margarine and sugars. Beat in vanilla and eggs. Add all dry ingredients, blending well. Stir in candy coated milk chocolate pieces. Drop by teaspoonsful onto cookie sheet. Bake at 350 degrees for 10 to 12 minutes until light brown. Let cool. Makes 6 dozen.

Trace your cookie cutter onto bright heavy paper. Cut out the shape and you have wonderful gift tags. They can also be accented with rubber stamps.

Carol Jones

El Bandito Cookies

Marty Darling

1 c. shredded sharp
  cheddar cheese
  (room temperature)
1 c. crispy rice cereal

3/4 t. cayenne pepper
1 stick margarine, softened
1 c. flour

After cheese and margarine are VERY soft, mix all ingredients together by hand until smooth. Roll out between waxed paper to 1/4" thickness and cut with cookie cutter (shape of Texas is great for these). Bake for 15 minutes at 350 degrees on cookie sheet.

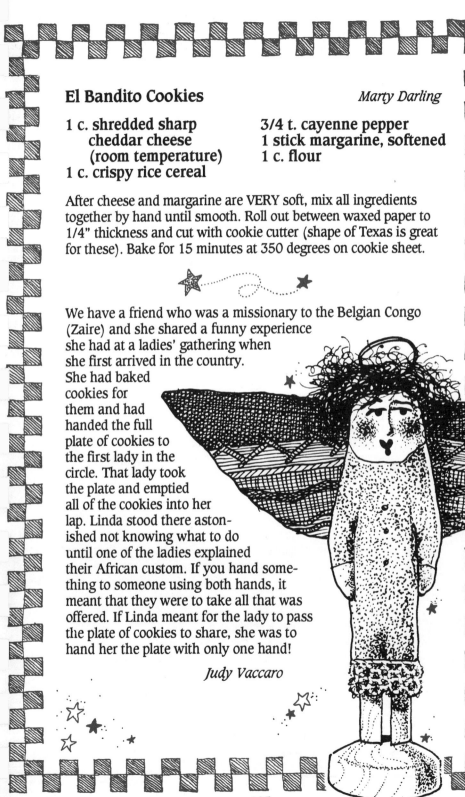

We have a friend who was a missionary to the Belgian Congo (Zaire) and she shared a funny experience she had at a ladies' gathering when she first arrived in the country. She had baked cookies for them and had handed the full plate of cookies to the first lady in the circle. That lady took the plate and emptied all of the cookies into her lap. Linda stood there astonished not knowing what to do until one of the ladies explained their African custom. If you hand something to someone using both hands, it meant that they were to take all that was offered. If Linda meant for the lady to pass the plate of cookies to share, she was to hand her the plate with only one hand!

Judy Vaccaro

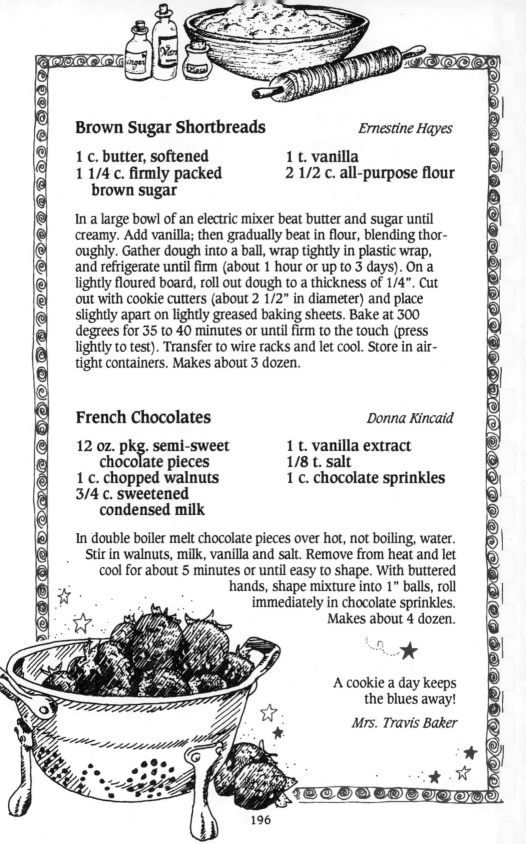

Brown Sugar Shortbreads

Ernestine Hayes

1 c. butter, softened
1 1/4 c. firmly packed
  brown sugar

1 t. vanilla
2 1/2 c. all-purpose flour

In a large bowl of an electric mixer beat butter and sugar until creamy. Add vanilla; then gradually beat in flour, blending thoroughly. Gather dough into a ball, wrap tightly in plastic wrap, and refrigerate until firm (about 1 hour or up to 3 days). On a lightly floured board, roll out dough to a thickness of 1/4". Cut out with cookie cutters (about 2 1/2" in diameter) and place slightly apart on lightly greased baking sheets. Bake at 300 degrees for 35 to 40 minutes or until firm to the touch (press lightly to test). Transfer to wire racks and let cool. Store in airtight containers. Makes about 3 dozen.

French Chocolates

Donna Kincaid

12 oz. pkg. semi-sweet
  chocolate pieces
1 c. chopped walnuts
3/4 c. sweetened
  condensed milk

1 t. vanilla extract
1/8 t. salt
1 c. chocolate sprinkles

In double boiler melt chocolate pieces over hot, not boiling, water. Stir in walnuts, milk, vanilla and salt. Remove from heat and let cool for about 5 minutes or until easy to shape. With buttered hands, shape mixture into 1" balls, roll immediately in chocolate sprinkles. Makes about 4 dozen.

A cookie a day keeps
the blues away!

Mrs. Travis Baker

Auri's Cookies (Dog Treats)

Katherine Gaughan

2 c. whole wheat flour
2/3 c. yellow cornmeal
2 T. corn oil
1/2 c. chicken broth

2 eggs mixed with
  1/4 c. milk
1 beaten egg

Combine flour, cornmeal, oil, broth and eggs with milk in order.
Let set for 15 minutes. Roll out to 1/4" thick. Cut into dog bone
shape and brush with beaten egg. Bake at 350 degrees for 30
minutes until golden.

Autumn Pumpkin-Oatmeal Cookies

Judy Hand

1 1/2 c. margarine
1 c. sugar
2 c. brown sugar
2 eggs
1 t. vanilla
4 c. flour

2 t. baking soda
1 t. salt
1 1/2 t. ground cinnamon
2 c. quick oatmeal
1 3/4 c. canned pumpkin
1 c. chocolate chips

Cream together thoroughly margarine and sugars. Add eggs and
vanilla, beat until fluffy. Sift dry ingredients (with exception of
oatmeal) and add alternately with the pumpkin. Stir in chocolate
chips and oatmeal. Drop by teaspoonsful onto a greased baking
sheet. Bake at 350 degrees for 8 to 10 minutes. This makes a
very large batch of cookies...10 dozen!

For really black frosting for Halloween
cookies, if you add some blue
food coloring to your chocolate
icing, it turns black.

Deirdre Burton

INDEX

Cookie Cutters · Cookie Gifts

Cookie Traditions

Cookie Ornaments

Cookie Memories

Cookie Garlands

Cookie Hints · Cookie Recipes

Cookie Cutters • Cookie Gifts

Cookie Traditions

Cookie Memories

Cookie Hints • Cookie Recipes

Cookie Garlands

Cookie Ornaments

Cookie Cutters · Cookie Gifts

Cookie Traditions

Cookie Memories

Cookie Hints · Cookie Recipes

Cookie Garlands

Cookie Ornaments

Cookie Cutters • Cookie Gifts

Cookie Traditions

Cookie Memories

Cookie Recipes • Cookie Hints

Cookie Garlands • Cookie Ornaments

Cookie Cutters • Cookie Gifts

Cookie Traditions

Cookie Memories

Cookie Hints • Cookie Recipes

Cookie Garlands

Cookie Ornaments

Cookie Cutters • Cookie Gifts

Cookie Traditions

Cookie Memories

Cookie Recipes • Cookie Hints

Cookie Garlands

Cookie Ornaments

We've cooked up a whole collection of Gooseberry Patch® books!

Have a taste for more? Call us toll-free at
1-800-854-6673

We'll send you our latest catalog filled with snowmen, Santas, ornaments, candles, cookie cutters, gourmet goodies, salt-glazed pottery collectibles and MORE...including our best-selling cookbooks!

Phone us:
1·800·854·6673

Fax us:
1·740·363·7225

Visit our website:
www.gooseberrypatch.com

Send us your favorite recipe!

*and the memory that makes it special for you!** We're putting together a brand new **Gooseberry Patch** cookbook, and you're invited to participate. If we select your recipe, your name will appear right along with it...and you'll receive a FREE copy of the book! Mail to:

Vickie & Jo Ann
Gooseberry Patch, Dept. BOOK
P.O. Box 190
Delaware, Ohio 43015

*Please help us by including the number of servings and all other necessary information!

Cookie Cutters · Cookie Gifts

Cookie Traditions · Cookie Memories

Cookie Ornaments

Cookie Garlands

Cookie Hints · Cookie Recipes